Non-Stop Inertia

Non-Stop Inertia

Ivor Southwood

Winchester, UK
Washington, USA

First published by Zero Books, 2011
Zero Books is an imprint of John Hunt Publishing Ltd., Laurel House, Station Approach,
Alresford, Hants, SO24 9JH, UK
office1@o-books.net
www.o-books.com

For distributor details and how to order please visit the 'Ordering' section on our website.

Text copyright: Ivor Southwood 2010

ISBN: 978 1 84694 530 4

A CIP catalogue record for this book is available from the British Library.

Design: Tom Davies

Printed in the UK by CPI Antony Rowe
Printed in the USA by Offset Paperback Mfrs, Inc

We operate a distinctive and ethical publishing philosophy in all
areas of our business, from our global network of authors to
production and worldwide distribution.

To my Mum and Dad

CONTENTS

Introduction   1
Non-Stop Inertia   7
Precarity 2.0   15
Emotional Labour   23
Non-Places   31
Virtual Mobility   37
From Unemployment to 'Jobseeking'   43
The Privatisation of Unemployment   49
Jobseeking as Career   57
Mind the Gap   63
Predictable Unpredictability   75
Ways Out   79
Notes   89

Introduction

Business at the warehouse was going downhill rapidly. There had already been meetings on the floor and warnings about dire times ahead. I'd only been taken on from the agency and made "permanent" a couple of months earlier, and already I was expecting to be got rid of. I'd been applying for new jobs continuously anyway since I had started there. But for others who were more attached to the place, its social and historical solidity was dissolving before their eyes. We knew that sooner or later there would be a huge cull which would eliminate about a third of the workforce; but in the meantime people were being given notice in dribs and drabs, two or three every month, mostly people like me who had only recently been employed. Every day could be the day you got the tap on the shoulder.

Meanwhile the managers strode along the aisles, on the lookout for people not keeping themselves occupied – the reductions in their own workloads presumably gave them more time for surveillance duties – and whenever one of them approached as I was dragging some pallet along or flattening a box I'd think, could this be my P45 moment? If I was being cynical I could suggest that some of the managers seemed to actually enjoy the tension that this atmosphere brought, and the extra power it gave them, even as they applied for other jobs themselves (interestingly, all the managers who seemed to embrace this role were also men). The disciplinary regime meant that no-one could stop working in the afternoon until one of the managers came out of the office and shouted at us that we could go. In the last few minutes of the day, rather than wind down naturally, people would sneak nearer to the door to make a quick getaway when the call came, hide behind the racking like naughty school-children in order to have a conversation, or simply make gestures of looking busy, sweeping up invisible dirt or tidying shelves, even if the real work, and the will to do it, had long since dried up.

What did we have to look forward to? The sale of the company to a group of venture capitalists and the subsequent charade of a "consultation"; being scored by managers on our work performance and having to score ourselves, and then discuss the disparity between these two ratings in an interview; re-applying for our jobs and being encouraged to sell ourselves back to the company in competition with our colleagues, even as we suspected that the decisions had already been made. The temptation to refuse to take part in this bleak pantomime was overruled by the impulse for survival. Many hard-working and experienced staff were shocked by the brutality of these exercises, which seemed designed to systematically attack their self-esteem. Again, while redundancies were inevitable considering the state of the company, the way the process was conducted, compounded by the pretence of openness and fairness, was almost deliberately humiliating.

One day, after we had been let out of the building many of us would soon be leaving forever, I overheard two colleagues talking a few seats behind me on the bus. Discussing the situation, a clever and sensitive man whose wry sense of humour helped make the place tolerable remarked to his friend that the best solution for all concerned would be for the North Koreans to drop a nuclear bomb on the place. His companion responded with a roar of laughter.

The fleeting image of obliteration summed up our own daily tasks of emotional fission: the ambivalence which irradiated the building, piercing our most mundane gestures with ridiculous unspoken fear, and the immense energy involved in splitting our real selves off from our work identities. We hated the place and despised everything it had come to stand for, and yet we were terrified of being "set free" into an economic vacuum where we would struggle to find work and have to present ourselves indiscriminately to other potential employers as similarly enthusiastic, compliant and flexible. I often arrived at the warehouse in the mornings with a mixture of relief that I still had a job and disappointment that the place had not been somehow swept away during the night, or hoping that the managers, knowing that their time was up, had deserted their posts like guards leaving a camp, so at last we could roam the aisles and offices freely without fear of reprimand until an executive somewhere remembered to phone a temp and order her to press a button and delete us all.

In a way, these contradictory but taken-for-granted feelings – a fear of imminent destruction and at the same time a wish for this corrupted and imprisoning system to collapse – form the starting point for this book. There is a sense of overwhelming precariousness, in work, in matters of money, and in culture generally; a feeling of being kept in suspense which appears like a law of nature, rather than something human-made. For many people the current economic "crisis" has arguably only validated this already-existing precariousness, and made it seem even more unchallengeable.

By exploring various aspects of culture, concentrating especially on the workplace and its related settings, I argue that this state of insecurity – which taps into our deepest fears and desires, much as neurosis draws on and distorts the unconscious – is artificially maintained, while being presented as inevitable, just a fact of life. A continual restless movement towards the next job, commodity or identity means that this reality never really comes into focus: our vision is always too blurred to orientate ourselves or see how things might be changed. Whether literally or figuratively, by way of temporary work and perpetual jobseeking or mobile media and aspirational consumption, this superficial movement conceals a deep paralysis of thought and action. Undercurrents of resentment at our enforced participation are suppressed by a daily deluge of positive language: interactivity, progress, opportunity, choice. For evidence of this one need look no further than the anxiety and depression lurking beneath the upbeat discourse of career flexibility, or the increasing amounts of time routinely spent job searching and commuting at the expense of interests outside work.

Although theoretical sources are used to back up its arguments, this book is not a detached academic study. It is written from within the debt-driven jobseeking subjectivity which it describes. Neither is it framed by a journalistic sabbatical after which the author returns to normal life; this *is* normal life, a predicament which is, in the current parlance of work, wars and crises, "ongoing". Theory is used to try to interpret various aspects of this everyday reality. In this way, I hope to bring into focus a social structure which at times seems both taken-for-granted and wilfully incomprehensible. To do this from inside, as it were, is a battle which has shaped the content of this book. Attempting to make sense of this absurd situation whilst in the grip of its demands is like trying to solve a Rubik's Cube at gunpoint; the gradual annexing of mental territory is arguably both the main source of conflict between the co-ordinators of work and their flexible operatives, and the means of its suppression. Some ideas are raised here about how to try to achieve a minimal critical distance from the arbitrarily assigned and tightly regulated role of precarious worker/jobseeker. If such opportunities for stability or space were already freely available then the book itself would not need to be written.

The book is organised as follows: chapters two, three and four are concerned with issues of context, outlining this culture of flexibility and asking whether it has provided opportunities to overturn the established order or just created new means of control. Here I also explore the concepts of "precarity" – a theoretical formulation of the work-related precariousness just described – and "emotional labour", a term pertaining to the widespread production of *feelings* in contemporary work. The next two chapters look at the transient "non-places" of commerce, transport and communication which frame so much of today's work and leisure, and challenge the conventional view that technological mobility has liberated the virtual worker. After this I deal with the blurring of boundaries between work and non-work, specifically through the movement from unemployment to "jobseeking", the privatised self-help discourse which is imposed on jobseekers, and the idea that as work been destabilised, jobseeking has become a career in itself. Chapters ten and eleven illustrate these interconnected themes by concentrating on a few of my own encounters with temporary work and its social effects; and finally, as mentioned above, I speculate upon some possible forms of resistance to this system which seems to pre-empt and neutralise traditional forms of opposition.

It will be seen, then, that the content of the book moves from a theoretical perspective informed by personal experience towards an account of personal experience informed by theory.

Non-Stop Inertia

From street level, among the debris of spent lottery tickets and crumpled talent show contestants staring up from the covers of discarded free newspapers, the period of apparent change and upheaval through which we are currently living seems to signify not the disintegration of the old forms of social inequality but the consolidation of them. Just as the "war on terror" has been used as a pretext for military violence and police surveillance, the everyday language of insecurity has been put to the service of maintaining structural security. The state of emergency seems to have been made permanent. Employers in the UK and elsewhere routinely impose competitive performance targets, use short-term contracts and rely on casual agency labour, and workers accept these arrangements along with their effects: continual stress, disrupted workplace relations and irregular income. Bank debts have been seamlessly transferred to the state while public services are squeezed; supermarket chains and energy companies rake in huge profits while their customers struggle to make ends meet. And the more individuals and communities are pulverised by these pressures, the more effective they become as raw material for re-pointing the capitalist brickwork.

How did things get to this stage, where such insecurities and anxieties are taken for granted, where opposition has been flattened and so many people's lives have been taken over by a zombie existence of debtworking and jobseeking? To begin to find out, it is instructive to go back to the time when such a situation really was new and strange. In 1988 cultural theorist

Stuart Hall attempted to come to terms with these "New Times", as they were briefly known. He offered a comprehensive list of the then emerging characteristics of this now all too familiar era, under the general heading of post-Fordism:

> more flexible, decentralised forms of labour process and work organisation; decline of the old manufacturing base and the growth of . . . computer-based industries; the hiving-off or contracting out of functions and services; a greater emphasis on choice and product differentiation, on marketing, packaging and design, on the 'targeting' of consumers by lifestyle, taste and culture rather than . . . social class; a decline in the . . . skilled, male, manual working class, the rise of the service and white-collar classes and the 'feminisation' of the workforce; an economy dominated by multinationals . . . the 'globalisation' of the new financial markets . . . greater fragmentation and pluralism, the weakening of older collective solidarities . . . the emergence of new identities associated with greater work flexibility, the maximisation of individual choices through personal consumption.[1]

These changes were mirrored, for Hall, by a reconfiguration of ourselves as subjects: the New Times "are both 'out there', changing our conditions of life, and in 'in here', working on us. In part, it is *us* who are being re-made." Challenging the traditional tactics of the socialist opposition as much as the governing strategies of capitalism, Hall argued that in this new climate a return to the old Fordist production line organisation of politics was impossible: society must instead strive to turn post-Fordism "inside out", appropriating new technology and embracing these "new social movements", finding "new points of antagonism" through "a politics of the family, of health, of food, of sexuality, of the body".[2]

This somewhat optimistic view of the possibilities of the new flexible era must itself be read in the historical context of a growing discourse of diversity, which was then beginning to challenge the old institutional structures of race and gender prejudice. The argument for a move from macro- to micro-politics represented an effort to divert the flow of the new liquefied culture, to claim the new politics of identity for those whose everyday lives had been routinely crushed by patriarchal-colonial capital.

Looking back on these New Times, however, it appears that the hopes of a new equality have not materialised. The endlessly innovative dimensions of post-Fordism mean that its inside-out version has proved to be just a logical progression of its dominant interests. In the UK, the new subjective politics antici-pated the seamless transition from Thatcherism to New Labour's lifestyle marketplace: the hollowing out of the public sector by the fake corporate language of "choice", the convergence of politics and media, a postmodernised menu of values dictated by consumption. Twenty years on, the rhetoric of diversity and empowerment has been largely incorporated into the business portfolio.

What is more, those same dominant interests which harvested the profits of the new flexibility have since succeeded in marketing fragmentation as a positive social aim, a quasi-Olympic project to which all citizens are required to contribute; so the contradictory logic of the micro-political New Times has been internalised. As Arlie Russell Hochschild notes, the ongoing capitalist project to commercialize intimate life expands not only globally, but also into the "local geographies of emotion".[3] The machinery has gone inside (literally in the case of the mood-regulating drugs so widely prescribed today).

Hall also looked forward to a new feminism, anticipating a move towards a "feminisation of the social";[4] however, one of the main achievements of the new lifestyle-politics has been to create a postfeminist subjectivity defined by consumerism, a position of what Nina Power has called "perky passivity".[5] Meanwhile the "soft skills" of negotiation and communication traditionally associated with feminised work have been reformatted by the cut and thrust discourse of business. (As a former NHS nurse I was somewhat taken aback during an interview, while going through my employment history, to hear the pinstriped recruitment agent describe nursing as a potentially "lucrative" profession.) Managers have found that when adapted for commercial use such skills make the perfect contemporary giftwrapping for old-fashioned inequality. Many of the lowest paid, most insecure and least valued jobs are still done by women, who are now merely talked down to in a more self-aware and slippery language than before.

Unsurprisingly for such an inside-out, back-to-front society, consent to this newly liberated/indebted way of life is manufactured through consumption. We are now addressed as consumers first and foremost, rather than producers, even if we are penniless: the illusion of choice must be maintained at all costs. Even the Jobcentre calls its claimants "customers". The role of unions in the public psyche has to a great extent been taken over by consumer rights groups. The globally positioned consumer-citizen is promised freedom and mobility through the wonders of the Internet, but this constant connectivity is in reality just another pressure. Digital consumption becomes an obligation, almost a form of self-care. Like unpaid technicians, we all obediently maintain our own media networks, and we are constantly contactable (especially by employers) through the miracle of the mobile phone, its de-yuppification another example of remote control disguised as liberation.

Permanent debt has come to shape this era of flexibility as much as insecure work, and the two are of course mutually supportive. Individual debt – due in many cases, including mine, to a combination of higher education and intermittent low-paid work, rather than the use of credit as a lifestyle-boosting steroid

– manoeuvres the individual into a position of complicity with the very system which is despised. A population submerged in debt is relatively easy to manage: most people cannot muster sufficient resources to maintain any real independence, while individual cases of financial or psychological disintegration are seen in corporate terms as an effective deterrent and a small price to pay for overall homeostasis.

Beneath the veneer of lifestyle choice, in reality most people cannot afford to accept or reject particular jobs according to their own ethical preferences or pursue outside interests which are not strictly "goal-oriented". Instead, both in and out of work one becomes a slave to one's own introjected boss, accepting even the most tenuous or unsuitable scraps of work, fulfilling one's duties of self-selling and availability, shopping at supermarket chains with unhealthy food and unhealthier employment practices and buying cheap Made In China goods. This suffocating indebtedness (along with the fear of terrorism) is the closest the UK population comes to having a collective identity. We hold our breath while a few oligarchs suck in the oxygen, even though we're supposedly "all in it together" ("it's up to all of us").

Such preoccupations divert attention away from wider abstract social or political concerns and onto a continual anxious self-surveillance. This constant precariousness and restless mobility, compounded by a dependence upon relentlessly updating market-driven technology and the scrolling CGI of digital media, together suggest a sort of cultural stagflation, a population revving up without getting anywhere. The result is a kind of frenetic inactivity: we are caught in a cycle of non-stop inertia.

From this vantage point, it is more important than ever to pull our gaze away from whatever new crisis/opportunity/spectacle is dangled in front of us and instead look for the reality which has re-installed itself in the digital/global network. Back in 1964 Herbert Marcuse described the "unfreedom" wrought by what he called a "one-dimensional society": a culture where opposition cannot take root and negativity is taboo, a discourse of liberation which contains within itself a code for continuing domination. This unfreedom has since found new means of exerting its power through precarious work, accelerated consumption, rolling media and technological individualization. These are the "new forms of control"[6] into which the New Times have coalesced.

Marcuse's text now reads more like prophecy than history, a warning of a synthetically smoothed out society geared entirely towards preserving authority through the elimination of friction and the dampening of conflict. "Thus emerges a pattern of one-dimensional thought and behaviour in which ideas, aspirations and objectives that, by their content, transcend the established universe of discourse and action are either repelled or reduced to terms of this universe."[7] Whether in politics, popular culture or academia, opportunities for real liberation today have indeed been largely repelled by market forces, or reduced to placatory simulations.

When this point is reached, domination – in the guise of affluence and liberty – extends to all spheres of private and public existence, integrates all authentic opposition, absorbs all alternatives. Technological rationality reveals its political character as it becomes the great vehicle of better domination, creating a truly totalitarian universe in which society and nature, mind and body are kept in a state of permanent mobilisation for the defence of this universe.[8]

We are permanently mobilised against change, recruited for the defence of the present economic universe. After a generation of New Times we are both exhausted by and inured to job insecurity and continuous availability, obligatory consumption and persistent debt; and we have become complicit in the system which perpetuates and reproduces these situations. Even as we struggle resentfully under the burden of this arrangement – which is somehow both ever-changing and unchanging – we maintain and disseminate it, regarding it as unavoidable and, in many cases, as perfectly natural. To break this cycle of passivity it is necessary once again to find new points of antagonism.

Precarity 2.0

The rootless worker cannot be uprooted. In an environment where jobs (or "assignments") appear and disappear at such a rate as to seem unreal, mundane everyday worries – home insecurity, debt, bureaucracy – are regularly amplified into supernatural threats by those who co-ordinate this environment. The dread which lies behind such taken-for-granted stress cannot be clearly defined but nevertheless seems to be a constant background presence. Daily life becomes precarious. Planning ahead becomes difficult, routines are impossible to establish. Work, of whatever sort, might begin or end anywhere at a moment's notice, and the burden is always on the worker to create the next opportunity and to surf between roles. The individual must exist in a state of constant readiness. Predictable income, savings, the fixed category of "occupation": all belong to another historical world.

It seems vital, then, to give a name and a shape to this amorphous fear which presents itself to the post-Fordised subject as a force of nature or as something emanating from inside the individual rather than a deliberate external arrangement of power; and some theorists of contemporary work, including the philosopher Paolo Virno, have indeed named this particular constellation of insecurities as "Precarity":

It is a fear in which two previously separate things become merged: on one hand, fear of concrete dangers, for example, losing one's job. On the other hand, a much more general fear, an anguish, which lacks a precise object, and this is the feeling of precarity itself. It is the relationship with the world as a whole as a source of danger. These two things normally were separated. Fear for a determinate reason was something socially governable while anguish over precarity, over finitude, was something that religions or philosophy tried to administer. Now, by contrast, with globalisation these two elements become one.[9]

Feelings of sudden existential vulnerability now come upon the individual as if from nowhere, in the midst of indifference, in the banal space of work; at the customer service counter, in a warehouse or call centre, as s/he services the remote needs of the globalised professional class in an almost colonial fashion. And this fear also follows the unanchored worker out of the nominal workplace and into the home: it fills gaps in conversations, is readable between the lines of emails, seeps into relationships and crevices of the mind. The precarious worker is then saddled with an additional duty: to *hide* these feelings.

Precarity is a term which has gained currency in the last decade through its use by various anti-globalisation and anti-capitalist protest networks, sometimes involving the appropriation of its religious associations (the word originates in Catholic terminology).[10] However the idea among some activists that post-Fordist capitalism must eventually topple under the weight of its own insecurities and liberate the so-called "precariat" seems less hopeful today, in the wake of a financial crisis which has resulted not in an ecstatic collapse but a new strength of authority imposed through the normalising of insecurity across work sectors. The recession of 2008/9 and the emerging era of mass institutionalised precarity might therefore prove to be a turning point for these movements.

In a particularly lucid critique of the discourse of precarity, Angela Mitropoulos questions both the convenient conflation of different types of so-called precarious worker whose interests might actually be in conflict, and the supposed novelty of the category itself: "On a global scale and in its privatised and/or unpaid versions, precarity is and has always been the standard experience of work in capitalism." Precarity, Mitropoulos suggests, is an established historical dimension of domestic work, agriculture, sex work, hospitality, building and retail, and has been around since long before the arrival of the digital precariat.[11] Indeed, during the early years of large-scale factory production Marx noted the "temporary misery" of workers successively swallowed by industry only to be expelled by each new innovation: "The uncertainty and instability to which machinery subjects the employment, and consequently the living conditions, of the workers becomes a normal state of affairs." The more surplus-value the workers produce for the capitalist to re-invest in labour-saving machinery, "the more does their very function as a means for the valorization of capital become precarious".[12] Personal as well as social crisis has been a constant companion to capitalism throughout its successive stages of production.

The articulation of precarity in recent years is rather due to "its discovery among those who had not expected it"; those who might previously have been shielded by the relative stability of Fordism. As union support evaporates in the new flexible/virtual workplaces[13] it becomes apparent that, as Mitropoulos says, this stability was the exception, not the rule.[14] Further, there is a risk that the hypertextual discourse of precarity might merely reproduce and conceal the old divisions, with a tier of highly vocal media operators claiming to speak for the voiceless under-class of largely female and/or migrant casualised workers.

What does perhaps distinguish post-Fordist precarity from its previous models is the way it is positively re-packaged by mendacious politicians and cost-cutting bosses as an unprece-dented form of liberation from a boring old job for life; work is now supposedly both an empowering lifestyle choice and a matter of individual responsibility. This illusion is backed up by an ideology of consumerist aspiration, and by the liquidizing of the welfare state. Under the self-help dictum, if you find yourself caught in the quicksand of precarity it is up to you to haul yourself out, without relying on the employer or the state to offer a branch to cling to. Similarly, the emphasis upon self-promotion, the re-making of identity as CV material, and the masking of anxiety by an act of enthusiasm regarding whatever new generic role and costume is thrown at the individual, are also part of this new positive precarity.

Rather than a simple unity of interests, it might now make more sense to talk of a spectrum of precarity. In the UK, for instance, those at the sharp end include low paid migrant workers tied to unscrupulous agencies and gangmasters,[15] whose experiences only tend to reach public awareness through tragedies such as the deaths of 23 Chinese cockle pickers at Morecombe Bay in 2004; and those without financial back-up who are forced to navigate the border-zone between work and welfare, often while coping with the added burden of illness or disability. For these people the blending of economic and ontological anxiety, as described by Virno, is complete: the most tenuous work assignment or encounter with state bureaucracy can become a matter of life or death. These groups might actually have less in common with the freelance creatives arranging carni-valesque protests on their behalf than with people in formerly secure jobs, often in large organisations (including public services), who have been subjected over recent years to a gradual heating-up of anxiety through the imposition of temporary contracts, reconfigurations and performance reviews, and their outsourced colleagues in the agency hinterland. It is between these groups, with their hugely varying living conditions and social networks, that common resentments might be identified and useful alliances formed.

A sort of low-level or latent precarity, as experienced by myself and many others, is now a fixture of everyday life, both taken-for-granted and uncanny, immanent and untraceable; a vague electrical hum, hardly worth mentioning, too trivial to be worth complaining about ("it'll only be for a while", "at least I have a job", "it's the same for everyone", "that's just the way things are"). Especially with the guillotine poised over public services today, this repressed anxiety is fast becoming the norm; jobs dissolve into *Apprentice*-style compete-or-die self-marketing exercises, with the social purpose of the institution practically forgotten.

This set-up perpetuates itself by neutralising opposition. The spiking of the most trivial work tasks with micro-doses of anxiety drains the precarious worker of the energy to resist; the constant moves preclude insights into the wider context or co-operation between workers, and the worker who does not "help himself", even at the expense of others, is seen as deserving to fail and to suffer. This mental pressure encourages a sort of exhausted indifference, a "going with the flow" and acceptance of unfreedom. With labour infinitely replaceable, gestures of rebellion are anyway seemingly useless. The aberrant individual would only damage himself, ruining his own chances, and the system would go on just as smoothly as before.

The cold hard corporate frame of precarious work, on which its human subjects are hung like so many generic uniforms, must be exposed in order to be dismantled. Unsurprisingly though, given its generally unspeakable status, there is a conspicuous absence of discussion of precarity in mainstream politics and a wilful denial of its reality in debates on employment issues; to address the detrimental effects of irregular low paid work would mean jeopardising the flexible labour flow upon which the state hopes to float its economic recovery. Media coverage, meanwhile, understandably tends to focus on blatantly unfair cases rather than the less sensational exploitation which routinely occurs "within the rules". Similarly, despite some reported successes,[16] unions often seem (again, understandably) ambivalent towards agency workers, perhaps tending to view them more as a threat to the security of their own members than as potential allies.

Precarity is like the dirty laundry of large organisations: chief executives and productivity gurus avert their nostrils from its negative consequences. It is hidden away from visitors, just as the company distances itself from its outsourced labour, even if it is conducted onsite. There is no attempt to address the issue, for example, in Alain de Botton's *The Pleasures and Sorrows of Work*, which sticks resolutely, even quaintly, to its discrete occupational format. The topic does not impinge upon the glacial narratives of de Botton's scientists, engineers, accountants and entrepreneurs: work is presented here as an eternal process of honing and specialisation rather than a game of generic musical chairs, a vehicle by which individuals pursue their dreams to absurd perfection, whether in the form of a biscuit or a painting or a balance sheet, rather than a nameless phantom which stalks them through dingy corridors, threatening to erase their identities.

The closest de Botton comes to confronting the sheer emptiness of contemporary work is in his time following a career counsellor, whose motivational therapy sessions with soon-to-be-redundant employees reveal a terrible bleakness in their sentimental positivity.[17] Generally, however, rather than offering a romantic and reassuring continuation of the mythic tradition of the noble craftsman into the age of globalised flexibility, de Botton's researches would have yielded a far more realistic picture of 21st century work through an observation over the same time period of one person doing just as many different jobs, regardless of personal interest or aptitude, while applying for twice as many more, for a fraction of the pay and none of the social status.

As de Botton and his specialists travel though a landscape of warehouses, offices and corporate fairs, the low paid jobs which keep these non-places running so smoothly for their professional managers and customers are only ever mentioned in passing, and are never subjected to sustained examination. See for instance the philosopher's chance meeting with a Turkish lorry driver in a Belgian car park, his furtive glimpse of two cleaners "laughing animatedly while they worked" in a hotel room, or his brief encounter with a Brazilian waiter whose visa is soon due to expire in the staff restaurant of a City of London accountancy office.[18] Precarity can only be detected between the lines of his text as a repressed theme, enacted by a supporting cast of logistical and hospitality staff who provide a mere human backdrop for the ensemble of star performers.

The façade of work as a place of fulfilment and a source of continuity and stability detracts attention both from its fundamental placelessness and from the true insecurity of its transient workers/non-workers. The force of this repression suggests a widely held if unconscious fear; that an acknowledgment of the real situation would break the illusion and bring the whole stage-set crashing down.

Emotional Labour

Through observing the flight attendants employed by a US airline in the late 1970s and early 1980s, in her book *The Managed Heart* Arlie Russell Hochschild arrived at a theory of "emotional labour", meaning "the management of feeling to create a publicly observable facial and bodily display". The emotional labourer is required to "induce or suppress feeling in order to sustain the outward countenance that produces the proper state of mind in others".[19] Hochschild's argument, informed by Marx's critique of capitalist production, is that the construction of the persona of the emotional labourer through training, supervision and customer expectations draws upon the personal material of relationships and domestic life and transforms this into a profitable commodity, in the same way that the worker was historically alienated from his physical labour-power by the factory owner.

The transformation of the worker into the caring, cheerful or sexy flight attendant (or conversely the harsh, uncaring debt collector) therefore constitutes a form of labour in itself, whether through the external "surface acting" of gesture, language and facial expression, or the "deep acting" which involves immersing oneself in the role, a process akin to the technique of method acting.[20] In these ways the worker-performer manufactures the final product: the desired emotional state in the customer. A large part of the effort of emotional labour is taken up with creating the impression that the act is itself natural and effortless, because to show that it is contrived would invalidate the exchange and spoil the product.

Hochschild's analysis of customer service work anticipates later critiques of post-Fordist employment, particularly that sub-category of Michael Hardt and Antonio Negri's "immaterial labour" concerned with what they call "the creation and manipulation of affect".[21] The performative element also connects it to Virno's concept of "virtuosity": the worker as a "performing artist".[22] As such the idea of emotional labour, with its interior-ising of production and re-making of identity, as well as its view of the workplace as stage set or theatre, might be usefully updated and expanded in discussing the experience of the immaterialized precarious worker.

As Hochschild notes in her 2003 afterword to *The Managed Heart*, emotional labour has developed in two divergent ways since her original study. On the one hand, automation has reduced many interpersonal exchanges to computerised simula-tions (a cashpoint or website "thanks" the customer, a digitally patched together voice "apologises" for a delay). On the other hand, she suggests, looking at the US labour market, jobs relating to the outsourcing of personal and family responsibilities (and the outsourcing of emotions?) have increased.[23] To these new outlets I would add the proliferation of what I would call remote emotional labour – media work, advertising and marketing etc., especially using digital technology – during the same period. These form a sort of virtual network of indirect emotional production.

Through automation and the parcelling out to other countries of the manufacturing of physical goods, and a corresponding increase in new immaterial products (the interior colonisation of identity and relationships alongside the expansion of the capitalist empire into new territories), post-Fordism has arguably outlived the traditional customer-facing model of emotional labour. Its scripts have become generalised, insinuating their way into the very fabric of everyday life. Explicit claims over the bodies of individual workers have been curtailed (one cannot imagine, for instance, an airline today getting away with submitting its attendants to the demeaning weigh-ins and "girdle checks" common in the 1960s and 70s[24]), just as the formulaic fictions of sales-talk are rarely believed any more, either by actors or audience, being replaced by a postmodern knowingness on both sides. But at the same time the implicit burden of emotional labour has extended far beyond the traditional spheres of sales or corporate hospitality. As consumers, feelings are foisted upon us whether we want them or not, and accumulate in our consciousnesses like psychic junk, so that eventually it becomes impossible to differentiate between the real memories and the corporate implants; and through work we are asked, as responsible citizens, to recycle and reproduce these emotion-commodities, to sell them on to others.

So there has been a diffusion of such affective labour: it functions as a sort of plug-in air-freshener to cover up the stench of precarity in every office and retail outlet, and has also spread into those areas such as health, education and welfare which had previously cultivated a "sincere", not-for-profit form of emotional labour distinct from the synthetic demands of business. In the flexible workplace the manager increasingly comes to take the position of the customer who must be satisfied, and to whom one has to continuously sell oneself. For the temporary agency worker the old distinction between employer and customer is practically eliminated.

Back in 1983 Hochschild defined emotional labour as predominantly female and, perhaps more problematically, middle class (while acknowledging the emotional duties assigned, for instance, to supermarket cashiers);[25] but these demarcations, if they ever really existed, have since dissolved, enabling the tasks of emotional labour to percolate throughout society and conjure a convenient illusion of a genderless, classless workplace. Performative elements are now integral to jobs which would not be thought of in themselves as particularly emotionally laborious. Even warehouse assistants and data enterers have to present themselves as aspirational and dynamic, to be "effective communicators" and to identify personally with the interests of the organisation. So regardless of whether the work itself is directly concerned with the production of affect, it contains elements of emotion management and virtuosity, both in covering over true anxieties and hostilities and in summoning a contrived enthusiasm and commitment.

Illustrating this move towards communicational production, Virno suggests in *A Grammar of the Multitude* that the old Fordist production line with its sign "Silence, men at work!" has been superseded by a new post-Fordist cognitive imperative: "Men [and Women?] at work here. Talk!"[26] But it should be added, this talk is strictly regulated so as to maintain the correct "mindset". Consequently *not talking* becomes as potentially disruptive as talking used to be. Indeed, under the flexible conformity of precarity, there is no end to the personal resources of the worker upon which the employer can draw in the service of the company. Manual workers, as Virno suggests, are encouraged to contribute ideas for improving efficiency which are then absorbed into official company policy, rather than being shared informally as ways of making the job easier.[27] Even if such exercises are of no practical use to the management (i.e. in streamlining staff levels), they still serve a symbolic and ideological function by eliciting consent under a banner of "participation". The same can be said for "huddles" and "team-building" exercises, which paradoxically promote an individualized workplace in which informal social contact is compulsorily directed towards formal corporate goals, rather than work being a mere setting for social life. So a performance of informality might actually disguise a formality which is all the more powerful for being unacknowledged; and this (in)formality, like the orientation of the precarious worker, is internalised and becomes self-perpetuating.

Finally, and crucially for my purposes, emotional labour can be broadened beyond the traditional boundaries of work and applied to the whole para-occupation of "jobseeking". The well-prepared candidate has already started "putting in the hours" prior to receiving a wage. The skills required to present oneself correctly to employers and generate future opportunities constitute a new untrammelled form of emotional labour, driven by insecurity, which leaks over into leisure and consumption and colonises the social life whose energy it has drained, transforming the home into an office and friendship into a promotional network.

The job interview is perhaps the most obvious example of this sort of unpaid emotional labour: here the candidate must appear sufficiently confident and enthusiastic to satisfy a selection panel assessing "presentation" and "personality", as if these were objective scientific criteria. (Some employers, no doubt tooled up with pop-psychological theories of body language, seem to pride themselves on their ability to tell instantly from the way an applicant enters a room whether they are suitable for the job, unaware of how fantastically ignorant such claims make them sound.) So the interview, regardless of the job, becomes a kind of talent show audition hinging on generic questions about change, teamwork etc. (the equivalents of the standard repertoire of *X Factor* ballads), while the interviewee must project an all-purpose positivity by extemporising around this script without revealing its artificiality. The candidate must project the right image and hit the right notes, and must put his "heart and soul" into every performance, even for the most dreary role.

Preparation for the interview therefore ceases to be about the actual content of the job and instead becomes a theatrical rehearsal, concerned primarily with costume, demeanour, eye contact, stage presence, learning one's lines. The character of the applicant must be placed within a seamless yet engaging narrative, and any outside interests incorporated into the work sphere (so for instance, for a retail job, an interest in films becomes "I like to keep track of all the latest DVD releases"). Above all, it is important to appear "natural". Actual experience is secondary to a willingness to blend in; to contribute to that collective suspension of disbelief which is vital to the smooth running of the contemporary workplace.

Neither is such unpaid emotional labour limited to the supposedly professional, highly motivated candidate, as depicted by the smiling replicants of agency websites and corporate newsletters. Under the law of aspirational inclusivity, everyone is a contestant in the jobseeking talent show, whether or not they are natural performers. The forced smile of compulsory enthusiasm is stretched across the welfare-to-work programmes and reflected in the unglamorous depths of the economy. I recently underwent a recruitment process for pre-Christmas shelf-stacking work at Asda (a UK subsidiary of Wal-Mart) which involved, first of all, filling in a multiple choice questionnaire ostensibly "designed to let us know more about the type of work you enjoy and the kind of person you are". This consisted of twenty pairs of either/or statements. Some examples:

A) I am orderly B) I am easy going
A) I am absorbed with ideas B) I notice things around me
A) I follow the rules B) I try to find short cuts
A) I am calm B) I am lively
A) I work best without pressure B) I enjoy time pressure
A) I am argumentative B) I respect authority

Of course the answers given say nothing about your personality, other than whether you understand the expectations of the workplace you will be entering, and whether you are willing to conjure up a version of yourself which fits in with that workplace – showing respect for order, rules and authority, and displaying enjoyment linked to productivity (Oh yes, I *enjoy* time pressure), supplying practical energy rather than calm absorption and abstract ideas. Many other retailers have similar recruitment questionnaires, whose pseudo-psychological blurb is merely a cover for testing one's capacity for conformity. The flimsy realism of the act is illustrated by the statement on the form that "there are no right or wrong answers". By circling the correct first-person statements and signing the form, the candidate "takes ownership" – in the current therapy-speak – of this ultra-complaint persona, gives it his name, and consents to its future on-demand production.

The questionnaire was followed by a "group screening" session in the training room of an Asda store. There twelve of us were shown a corporate documercial in which various beaming employee-performers listed the company's "values" and "beliefs" (unsurprisingly, these involved saving its customers money and looking after its employees, rather than making money for itself out of those customers and employees). We were then divided into groups, given large sheets of paper and coloured pens, and told to design a poster, based on the content of the video, which would "sell" Asda to a potential employee. Finally, each group had to stand up and present its poster to the other groups and the assessors.

It might seem odd to approach retail recruitment from the point of view of promoting the company to its own staff, rather than to its customers; but then, as noted earlier, this process is not so much about "selling" in the old sense, but about instilling a particular way of performing-thinking-feeling; making the candidates claim this positive attitude as their own and recognise it in others, as something natural and almost spiritual, rather than artificially imposed.

Under cover of a teamwork exercise, this was effectively a task of emotional labour. We were required to induce and suppress certain feelings in such a way as to satisfactorily identify Asda/Wal-Mart as the caring happy "family" of the corporate video, presumably with the managers cast as parents and ourselves as innocent children, in a felt-tipped primary coloured world where the reality of consumer capitalism was unthinkable, or at least unspeakable. As with the questionnaire, this exercise (which, behind the façade of "selection", was surely self-eliminating) demanded an act of virtuosity, using various props to improvise the sort of generic character which was expected of us - positive, unquestioning, enthusiastic, extra-mile-going - and then offering this version of ourselves willingly. The aim was to plant in our minds a suitable emotional orientation which could later be harvested for a profit.

Non-Places

This sort of performative labour is typically enacted on an ever-expanding stage-set of "non-places", as anthropologist Marc Augé describes them: a programmed landscape of retail parks, travel networks, leisuredromes and virtualized call centres which could be anywhere or nowhere, transitional spaces of communication and consumption which contain people "in the manner of immense parentheses".[28] Indeed the non-place commuter/consumer might only become fully aware of the reality of such spaces and the people who work in them[29] at moments of crisis or breakdown, when a journey is short-circuited by a technical failure or the spell is broken by a security alert. It is only when stranded and immobilised that people actually start to notice these interspaces which seem designed to be passed through as if in a dream. Manuel Castells identifies these liminal zones, along with the electronic corridors of cyber-space, as representations of "the space of flows". Such space is somehow amnesic as well as placeless. "Localities become disembodied from their cultural, historical, geographical meaning, and reintegrated into functional networks",[30] given over to the wholesale global circulation of information and capital.

The identity of the person who passes through the non-place is similarly wiped, plugged into the media hub and filled with a predetermined set of images, immaterial products and services. As Augé puts it: "the space of non-place creates neither singular identity nor relations; only solitude, and similitude."[31] The non-place is safeguarded by its own array of passwords and CCTV cameras and governed by its own rules of costume, gesture and language which mediate the transactions between the virtual consumer and the non-place worker. In the recent film *Up in the Air*, when the perpetually mobile executive played by George Clooney swipes his business card at the airport the check-in clerk is instructed to give him a specific pre-scripted greeting: "Pleasure to see you again, Mr Bingham." This world of "simulated hospitality" contrasts with the real business of informing employees of major US companies that they are being made redundant. The hotel lifestyle which the character enjoys is soon revealed as a way of preventing this depressingly human aspect of his job from weighing him down.[32]

Through their generic and transient qualities – workstations devoid of personal effects, relations with colleagues as fleeting as those with passengers on a commuter journey – many workplaces now resemble non-places, either literally, as in the case of a hotel, corporate coffee chain or out-of-town supermarket, or symbolically, in the form of temporary assignments for faceless employers (dis)located in anonymous buildings, where the worker-commuter then follows the same global timetables, navigates the same software applications and experiences the same sense of place-lessness, the feeling of being mere data in the mainframe.

Communication in these work(non-)places is also more likely to be personal*ised*, rather than personal. Face-to-face interaction is eschewed in favour of remote communication. The reliance upon email exchanges, even between colleagues in the same office, creates gaps between message and reply which would not be possible in spoken conversation, thereby evading direct contact and possibly even re-establishing old hierarchies under cover of networked informality. The junior staff member can send a question, but the manager can choose when to respond, if at all; temporary staff might be excluded from the email system altogether.

The temp or outsourced worker is also in a non-place in terms of status, existing in a grey area between other assignments or between employer and agency, perhaps making do with a borrowed uniform or desk ("here, you can use this while so-and-so's away") and a job description which is likely to be similarly arbitrary and anonymous. Even at work, the temporary worker has not really *arrived*. I was once given a temporary admin job in an edge-of-town office compound adjoining a bypass. After a few days of filling in spreadsheets I arrived for my five-hour shift to be told that due to a computer fault, there was no work for me. The company had phoned the agency and asked them to contact me at home to tell me not to bother coming in, but by that time I'd already left. Bound by the self-censorship brought on by the need for positive references, I smiled and accepted this gracefully. I was told to come back the next day, which I dutifully (or dumbly) did, when I was given half an hour of brochure-packing and then told that the work had dried up. For the last two days I had driven out to this peripheral site only to hang around in a sort of waiting room, in case my services were required, and then leave again.

Clearly this kind of arrangement would not be so easily tolerated by someone employed directly by the company, but this not to say that permanent workers are immune to the traffic flow of the non-place, subjected as they are to frequent changes of job title and location and constant pressure to re-apply for roles. In an environment of hotdesking, weak social ties and short-term projects, it seems that any evidence of attachment to place or identity is regarded as a form of bacteria which must be regularly swept away to keep the work surfaces clean and hygienic.

All work-space is now susceptible to the amnesic influence of the non-place, with its open-plan anonymity (no privacy, but no social structure either) and reduction of relationships to transferrable data. Some public sector employers invite private consultants to examine their work-flows and recruit specialist "Business Change Managers" to implement ongoing reconfiguration programmes. Since 2004 the official name for the NHS's scale of pay and conditions has been "Agenda for Change", as if insecurity should define the very core of the institution as well as the jobs it outsources to private suppliers. Where high staff turnover and fragmentation in public organisations used to be regarded as liabilities, now they are presumably seen as assets, enhancing corporate flexibility regardless of the detrimental impact upon service provision.[33]

So the "multi-faceted, generalised flexibility" of the network society[34] has its downside: a free-floating precariousness created by this rootless approach to work which shadows the flow of information and labour through public and virtual spaces and which, if acknowledged at all, is presented as inevitable or even positive. Under the ultra-competitive operating system of Precarity 2.0, the sense of imminent catastrophe which was once seen as a symptom of a dysfunctional workplace has been re-launched as an incentivizing strategy, even in supposedly non-commercial organisations. Once installed in the workplace, of course, this anxiety-system has to be maintained, like any other piece of machinery. As demonstrated by the email-obsessed office or interminable call centre, in many ways the informational era has engineered a repression of real social conflicts by a new bureaucratic system which endlessly circulates anxieties rather than confronting and resolving them.[35]

The digital workplace is also now conveniently portable and no longer restricted in terms of space or time. Technological innovation has created new mobile precarity devices: there is no escape from the discourse of liberation. For most people "work/life balance" is not a Sunday supplement vision of harmony and enjoyment, but rather an ongoing war against an alien force which threatens to vaporise them, and letting work roam free in the open sphere of social and personal life creates an all-pervasive 360 degree anxiety. The culture of flexibility and mobility paradoxically imposes an ever-tightening grip on the individual who is always accessible by mobile phone, email or laptop, while at the same time this culture is re-packaged as a gateway to leisure, sold through an Advertopia of "seamless connectivity".[36]

Perhaps the most vivid dramatisation of this placeless anxiety is 24 hour news. With its pumping and draining of personalities and monitoring of vital signs, digital news depicts the world as a continually unfolding narrative of non-places – business zones, transport terminals, entertainment complexes, the news studio and the Internet themselves – upon which the multi-platform precarity of everyday life is enacted and its blurred perspective reproduced. There is now no time to assess a news story from a critical distance, because the reporter has to comment on the event "as it happens" (or even *before* it happens) and improvise to fill the space, using speculation or viewer-supplied material (the outsourcing of news) if necessary. This is the media equivalent of "looking busy".

The flow of rolling news in the era of terrorism and economic meltdown lends a new ambiguity to what Raymond Williams described back in 1973 as television's "grabbing of attention in the early moments" and "reiterated promise of exciting things to come, if we stay."[37] An apocalyptic tension is communicated through the threat (or promise?) of imminent narrative overload conveyed by the ominous screen-tickers and the extemporised language of the presenters. The combination of speculation and improvisational staging means that in the absence of any real catastrophe, the graphic and verbal signifiers of crisis soon become attached to tawdry non-events. Again superficial movement disguises an underlying stasis. As the "BREAKING NEWS" tag scrolls across the screen yet again, accompanied by images of scandalised sports stars or blank-faced politicians, one can't help thinking that while this story is being covered in microscopic detail, somewhere something far more important *isn't* happening.

Virtual Mobility[38]

There is of course an aspirational element to this oxymoronic fixation with mobility, the idea conveyed by motivational experts that in our great society of classless opportunity anyone who puts in the effort can make it to the top (without explaining why there still is a "top" to "make it" to). The trouble is that in the current culture of sink-or-swim individualism it is not just upward mobility which relies upon an extracurricular regime of self-marketing, off-the-job training and networking, but also the meagre business of keeping afloat. What was once a Filofax fantasy has now become a universal requirement. Since the old boundaries which restricted and defined work in terms of time and space have been removed, there is no longer any refuge from the climate of careers. The enterprising individual simply has to immerse himself in this new virtual environment, just as he does in his professional role.

This can be illustrated by some excerpts from a typical entrepreneurial self-help manual, in which the author celebrates the flattening of the old workplace in favour of the new mobile technological space of flows:

> Business success is not about specialism, it's actually about juggling a number of talents. And forget Work/Life Balance, it's more Work/Play Integration, it's about mixing 'It' all up. [. . .] I was out for a day of meetings and put an auto responder on my email saying 'I am out of the office'. *'What do you mean, you are out of the office?'* shouted back a reply from my friend

David, 'YOU ARE YOUR OFFICE.' And he's right; work is no longer somewhere we clock in and out of; it's a mindset that we dip in and out of. [. . .] Different places can help reflect the multi-dimensional you. You'll have your office, perhaps a workspace at home, favourite coffee shops where you do certain things and weekend places where you do others . . . We are nomadic, working from airplanes, trains, wherever. There are no rules and no walls to where and how we work.[39]

This sort of "I've done it, so can you!" success-bible sub-genre preaches total availability as total liberation: "no walls and no rules". The interiorisation of work and its takeover of identity – "you are your office", the correct "mindset" etc. – are described as the path to the "multi-dimensional you". (Ironic, then, that to pick up such books is to step into a profoundly *one-dimensional* world of empty positivity.) This model of work is somehow not only blissfully enjoyable, but generic and immaterial, purely a matter of dynamic flow and effective communication.

These career makeover manuals and their TV equivalents advertise a frictionless lifestyle towards which the overworked self-employee or somnambulant non-place traveller is supposed to aspire; they sell the idea of transforming the arbitrary world of waiting rooms and service stations into ideas-factories where one can "make things happen". The key to this upward mobility is the mythic integration of work and play (encapsulated by that dreadful neologism, "weisure"), by which the old restricting office is transformed into an open-plan Utopia of creative connectivity. Utopia itself is of course the definitive non-place, an imaginary destination signposted by mobile phone companies and fashion retailers and encoded in the synthetic smiles of a thousand airbrushed fashion models plastered over the grim purgatory of the commuter grid.

Alternatively, despite the rhetoric of creativity and fulfilment, one could view this sort of freelance entrepreneur as merely a button-pushing manager in a large commercial organisation, flitting between departments and calling upon junior staff – waiters, drivers, IT technicians etc. – to service his needs. Again, like the weightless businessman in *Up in the Air*, these executives exist exclusively in the space of flows, gliding through non-places as if in a virtual reality simulation. Their work is defined in terms of communication, but in fact they have embraced alienation as their true vocation.

Also slotting into this circuit of aspirational mobility, interestingly along old gender-power lines – although of course any suggestion of patriarchy would be refuted as a leftover of a more rigid, analogue age – is the "Virtual Assistant", whose job of taking on administrative work, arranging appointments, sending emails etc., is a re-invention of the personal assistant / secretary role for the online remote-working era. The main differences are that these mostly female Virtual Assistants (or VAs) tend to work from home rather than a conventional workplace, and instead of being employed by a single company with a definite boss they are typically freelance, with a portfolio of business "clients" whom they regard as partners and professional equals rather than employers. Indeed, their work requires a high level of technological and organisational skill which may be beyond those clients.

In contrast to the free-floating mobile executive who is out and about on planes and in cafés, however, the home-working Virtual Assistant is more likely to be having to "juggle" (that word again) work assignments, childcare and domestic chores. In a radio interview[40] one Virtual Assistant talks enthusiastically about her new career, and how she fits work into her home life. Setting herself up as a freelance VA after a career as an office manager was "scary" but also "exciting", and she is keen to distinguish the professional relationship with her clients – who include an independent financial advisor and that delightful term, a "headhunter" – from the old conventional boss-PA arrangement. She relishes the opportunity to "be my own boss" and, needless to say, "no two days are the same". In addition to her assisting duties, which she performs in between caring for her small child, she explains that she has to set aside time for "networking" and uses Facebook, Twitter and online forums to promote herself and attract more business. Being self-employed, arranging time off is obviously more difficult than in a traditional job. The VA interviewed above could not afford to leave her business for long, even after the birth of her child, as "clients still had to be taken care of". Who would cover her workload? Certainly not those clients, nor any colleagues, as these would now be redefined as competitors.

So here again technological mobility puts a new glossy cover on old social restrictions and reformats inequality as equality. In an early newspaper article on the topic, which paints another unsurprisingly positive picture of a day in the life of a Virtual Assistant, the VA tells the journalist: "My clients know that I am a self-employed businessperson, just like them . . . They are paying me to do specific tasks, and often things that they struggled to find the time to do on their own, so they are very appreciative."[41] Exactly how doing those tasks that clients don't have the time or inclination to do themselves is more empowering than say, traditional secretarial work, or contract cleaning, is not clarified. It is rather a pretence of equality: an act made more plausible by a mutual language of Microsoft applications and corporate jargon, and by the remoteness and mediation of the relationship, which, despite the home-office webchats, can conceal vastly differing personal circumstances just as effectively as an office door and intercom.

UK VAs have their own professional networks (online, obviously), such as the UK Association of Virtual Assistants, which seems to fulfil a double function of providing resources and advertising its members' services, for an annual fee. On its homepage this website greets business owners as potential customers, listing the advantages of taking on a Virtual Assistant. "You may not need a full time, or even part time employee but just require someone for occasional or limited secretarial services," the site suggests, before helpfully pointing out some of the hassles which can be avoided by hiring a VA over a full-time administrator:

> Then there are the employer's responsibilities, employees are entitled to sick pay, maternity leave and paid holiday and often seek generous benefits packages. It is estimated that the true cost of an employee is over double and often up to triple the cost of their annual salary in terms of benefits and liabilities. [...] Wouldn't it be perfect if you had a business assistant that was always ready to work for you, but only when you need them? Providing secretarial services from their own home or office, using their own equipment? Meet the Virtual Assistant (VA), an invaluable new work force that provides a practical solution for small businesses owners. [sic] A VA frees up your valuable time so you can concentrate on the important things that only you can do in your business.[42]

That's quite a subtle way to sell empowerment and equality in the workplace to your "clients".

The case of the Virtual Assistant shows how, under the rule of virtual mobility, entrepreneurial language can be applied to an essentially subordinate role[43] and a positive lifestyle discourse can be hooked up to a ruthlessly lean business model. The Virtual Assistant is the boss's disposable flexible friend; and once that boss is dispersed across a rolling network of virtual clients, he is harder to identify and challenge as a single figure, just as the assistants are themselves de-collectivised. It is also significant that the online networks which take the place of an actual workplace here combine social support and self-promotional activity. Co-workers are also rivals, and looking for work becomes indistinguishable from doing work. Through the need to continually drum up business, jobseeking is incorporated seamlessly into the job, as just another duty of communication and emotional labour. Meanwhile home itself becomes a kind of non-place, susceptible to the same timetables and rules of efficiency as an office.

As this model of work gains ever more prominence, as fixed premises and traditional jobs are subsumed into the space of flows and flexible contracts, there is the prospect of this sort of remote-controlled labour spreading out from the entrepreneurial sphere to become the norm. The supposedly classless society of the future might well arrange itself around an elite of WiFi managers serviced by a mass of virtual assistants who are kept occupied well beyond their nominal work duties. This will be a society where self-marketing is just another administrative task, employment involves fitting multiple differently shaped assignments into every available gap, and there is no real beginning or end to the working day; a world in which we are all either willing or reluctant jugglers.

From Unemployment to 'Jobseeking'

At the factory and workshop gates you would find dozens of
men waiting for a door to open and someone to step outside
and shout, 'One man'. There would be such a scramble, worse
than any rugby match, to get to that door. It reminded me of
the jungle – the survival of the fittest. It was a wonder the
people did not revolt. I suppose revolt was not thought of.
Men were kept too busy trying to find work.[44]

As noted earlier, the human marketplace of precarity and casual
employment is not new, as illustrated by the above excerpt from
an account of unemployment in Manchester in the early 1900s.
The "industrial reserve army" has always been a part of the
expanding business of capitalism: a proportion of the working
population is constantly being, in Marx's ironic words, "set free",
left out in the wilderness until industry finds new ways to
exploit them and they are called up for front line duties once
again.[45]

It might seem absurd to those like myself who are subjected
to the Kafkaesque bureaucracy and Orwellian surveillance of
today's Jobcentre, with its unseen "Decision Makers" and neigh-
bourhood spy hotlines, but the Labour Exchange was originally
introduced in the UK a hundred years ago as a way of making
life easier, rather than harder, for the unemployed. The intention
was to help them to conserve the energy otherwise needlessly
consumed in tramping from one factory gate to another by
allowing the work instead to come to them. The Labour

43

Exchange signified the recognition of unemployment as a public rather than a private problem, for which society, rather than the individual, was responsible. Instigated by social reformer William Beveridge, it was the first step towards a national system of unemployment benefit and a forerunner of the post-war welfare state.

Now, of course, after a generation of New Times and the unstitching of the social fabric by privatisation and debt, the welfare state has itself been deemed an unnecessary drag on the new corporate agenda, like a veteran factory worker for whom the managers affect a superficial public respect while secretly despising what he stands for and quietly pushing him out of the back door. After a brief interval of civilisation, the law of the jungle is being re-instated. Despite the widespread business closures and the bodies piling up once again in the Jobcentres, unemployment is now once again regarded as a matter of individual rather than social responsibility. The scramble for work, like much of the work itself, has been virtualized (the applicant can now tramp from home, scrolling through website after website); but the suppression of revolt and the grip of capital over the lives of "jobseekers" is arguably as strong now as it was in the days before the Labour Party and the Labour Exchange, both institutions having been postmodernised out of existence. As work is immaterialized, so is competition for it; the aggressive marketing of oneself is as crucial now as brute physical force would have been in the past in bringing one casual worker to the foreman's attention above the others.

In the 1980s the new era of globalisation and privatised "wealth creation" condemned many people to a lifetime on the dole. But this abandonment had the unintended consequence of cultivating by its very neglect a subculture of resistance, and set out a clear distance between those who bought into the new aspirational lifestyle and those who did not. This oppositional attitude was evident in popular culture, as for instance in The

Smiths' "Heaven Knows I'm Miserable Now" (1984), a song now often lazily misread as autobiographical angst. The activities listed by the "miserable" narrator – work, conjugal sex, getting drunk – were all things which lyricist Morrissey, as a dissident pop star and follower of socialist aesthete Oscar Wilde,[46] claimed that he *didn't* do. The words describe someone trapped in a cycle of mindless drudgery and equally mindless leisure, from which the dole could be a liberation: "I was looking for a job and then I found a job, and heaven knows I'm miserable now / In my life why do I give valuable time to people who I'd much rather kick in the eye?" The lyric suggests that misery frequently arises from chasing those normative signs of status and success which we are told will make us happy, and implies an alternative route to fulfilment through refusing to surrender to those illusions.

But this distance between the dominant ideology and its alternatives has since shrunk down to nothing. The dole-art interzone has been "regenerated", and all traces of rebellion have been sandblasted away. By the post-recession 1990s there could be no outsider position anymore, no opposition to the market; again the reserve army was called up and everyone's presence was required in the big corporate hospitality tent, either propping up the bar or serving behind it. Even those who did not particularly want to live the aspirational dream were forced to go with the flow. In the UK, the Tories swept up the jobless and funnelled them into "job clubs", and finally in 1996, formalising this new all-inclusive positivity, the unemployed were re-signified as "jobseekers" and Unemployment Benefit was re-branded as "Jobseeker's Allowance". And if that didn't convey the positive message strongly enough, the ideological prod of the "Plus" suffix was added to Jobcentres, as if to say: look, we're giving you even *more*, so there's even *less* excuse.

The re-branded jobseekers should always be seeking work, somehow instinctively, like pigs searching for truffles. "Jobseeker": a more demeaning label is difficult to imagine. It recalls a childish game of hide and seek, and the unemployed are indeed often treated like errant children who need to be kept in line by playground supervisors who make sure they go back into class promptly when the bell rings. There is also the spiritual connotation of "seek and ye shall find": if you do not find a job this is not a reflection of any real social situation, it is simply a failure of faith on your part; you just do not really *believe*.

The only labour now exchanged at the Jobcentre is the performative sort: empty gestures, feigned enthusiasm, containment of hostility, suppression of resentment. The "customer" and "advisor" are required between them to conjure an interaction which is entirely fake, a form of surface acting stretched over the underlying reality of compulsion and surveillance. Posters and leaflets in the Jobcentre depict smiling figures in work-like scenarios, proffering handshakes or clutching official-looking folders. The discourse of customer service adopted by the staff presents an illusion of empowerment, as if the claimant were choosing to buy a product, and deflects any real criticisms of the system onto pseudo-issues of standards or quality.

To refuse to go along with this performance and its mutual suspension of disbelief risks bringing the full weight of the institution down on the "customer"; he is reminded of his legal obligations and low status. An extraordinary depth and specificity of information is demanded from claimants on their efforts to find work: which newspapers have you looked in, which websites have you checked? Which employers have you contacted, about which jobs? "The more detail you give the better." All this must be written in the "Jobsearch Diary", which must then be handed over at every appointment, like a child's homework exercise, complete with patronising headings: "what I did – when I did it – what I will do next". Claimants are told they must do at least "three positive things per week", otherwise they could be referred to a Decision Maker and their benefits might be stopped. Evidence must be provided to "show us what you've done . . . so that we can see that you're doing enough to look for work."[47]

Occasionally a particularly officious advisor will go through all these details at an appointment and enter them into a database. Mostly, however, due to the current high levels of claimants, the staff do not have the time (or inclination?) to actually read what jobseekers have written in these compulsory diaries, or to comment on them – often I could have written "Disneyland Ride Operator" or "Time Travel Assistant" without attracting the least reaction – but still they must be filled in and submitted. The content of the text is of no consequence; what matters is the performance, the *act* of positivity.

Similarly, despite the regime of appointments, there is no real *discussion* of anything at the Jobcentre; any apparent discussion turns out to be an illusion, and an opportunity for the network of bureaucratic power to extend itself. The slightest forced expression of interest in, say, IT training, is immediately formalised into a two hour appointment with some pseudo-educational provider, from which one can then only extricate oneself at risk of being accused of shirking one's jobseeking duties. The advisors are not really there to dispense advice but rather to enforce authority. In this sense they are merely plain clothes versions of the private Group 4 security guards who routinely patrol Jobcentres today, looking out hopefully for the slightest signs of agitation. As if to reciprocate, the guards perform minor administrative duties and greet claimants, demonstrating that they are part of the same "helpful" service.

As I have found on several occasions over the past few years whilst having to justify to the Jobcentre my surplus existence as if defending my own case in some interminable trial, the stigma-tising effect of its thinly veiled interrogatory discourse is felt personally as an irrational sense of guilt. The ideological apparatus of the Jobcentre routinely interpellates[48] the claimant as lazy or wilfully inadequate if not downright fraudulent, and under such pressure even the most conscientious or self-assured person would struggle not to internalise this image. If the Jobcentre does indeed hail the benefit claimant as a customer, it is that type of shop where, having been monitored suspiciously by staff for signs of shoplifting, one feels obscurely intimidated and leaves the premises convinced that the theft alarm will go off, even if one's pockets are empty.[49]

The Privatisation of Unemployment

The Jobcentre Plus is merely the public showroom of this positive era of jobseeking. In 1998 the UK's New Labour government, carrying on where the Tories had left off, launched the "New Deal", paying private firms to run compulsory welfare-to-work training schemes in which the long-term unemployed (six months for those aged under 25, eighteen months for those over) were instructed in job searching skills and sent on work placements. The authorities had the power to withdraw benefit from those who did not attend such programmes or who refused "reasonable employment". This outsourcing of the reserve labour force was the next stage of post-Fordist governmentality: after the privatisation of public utilities, the privatisation of unemployment.

As well as its obvious economic aspects, this process of privatisation also involves the transformation of social causes of unemployment (and the social worthlessness of much actual work) into perceived individual inadequacies, which must be addressed as such in terms of discipline and rehabilitation. Unemployment is turned into a pastiche of a job, complete with mock workplace, clocking in and out times, and managers to report to; and the jobseeking subject, having being brought under the punitive authority of a private agency, is correspondingly privatised, both threatened with withdrawal of welfare and force-fed the aspirational discourse.

In 1999 a sociological study was made of a comparable welfare-to-work scheme in the US which targeted single mothers (the 1996 Personal Responsibility and Work Opportunity Reconciliation Act made receipt of welfare benefit conditional upon attendance at such schemes). Observing several courses of this scheme over a period of months, Anna Korteweg noted that the women were interpellated as "masculine worker-citizens" who were practically and morally obliged to seek work both as individuals and as role models for their children. The course concentrated on the need for the attendee to construct a self-image which would be attractive to employers, and conveyed a narrative of workplace success which many participants found to be rooted more in fantasy than reality.[50]

The staff who run such schemes are paid bonuses for those they manage to get into any sort of work, so each unemployed person is eyed as a potential cash prize. It is not surprising then that in this case the unemployee, perceived as an anonymous unit to be shifted, was subjected to a narrow and aggressive discourse of "'one-size fits all' individualism": failure to find a job was narrowed down to a series of generic "personality traits" addressed through various exercises, while social issues and personal histories were overlooked or subordinated to the jobseeker identity.[51]

Similarly, today the well-rehearsed UK media story of claimants being better off on benefits conveniently ignores the other side of the coin: that for many people, especially parents with the added burden of childcare, low paid work does not deliver a living wage. The subjects in Korteweg's study were primarily identified not as full-time mothers but as inactive employees. If motherhood or running a home were acknowledged at all, it was simply a "transferrable skill", something to add to the résumé to help the women market themselves more effectively as potential workers.[52]

An intensification of this mechanism of social privatisation is evident in a later study of a state-sponsored voluntary job searching support group among unemployed US college graduates. This group was seen by Ofer Sharone as functioning according to a "self-help paradigm":

Job seekers are encouraged to approach their search as their new job and to bring to it the same professional demeanour, discipline, and work ethic typically accorded to paid work . . . job seekers must exude a positive and optimistic attitude throughout the job search process. . . . Succeeding in the job of job searching is fully within the control of the individual job seeker. . . . external obstacles outside the control of the job seekers are either ignored or framed as surmountable given the right strategy.[53]

The job of job searching is here likened to a sales role, with members encouraged to look at themselves "as a product that I am selling" or as "the CEO of your own company that is in the business of selling yourself." This self-selling component of the job of job searching is maintained through the constant honing of presentational speeches which act as "personal commercials", and an emphasis upon social networking. Sharone identifies this as an extension of the duties of emotional labour, as defined by Hochschild; again there is a transfer of feelings from the personal to the corporate realm.[54] The potential employer is also the customer to whom one is trying to sell one's labour, so identity is therefore re-packaged as a promotional device for interviews, résumés etc., designed to instil a positive feeling in this employer-customer. For the endlessly flexible and instantly recruitable jobseeker, the transition from applicant to operative is seamless. The unpaid emotional labourer who demonstrates a high level of commitment to the corporate ethos is rewarded by being promoted to a paid role.

Clearly there is a potential disjunction here between the person's inner feelings (about a specific application, their previous work history, or their future prospects) and the positive gloss they are expected to put on these, both in managing their thoughts and in acting appropriately. As Sharone notes, once a certain number of carefully tailored résumés have disappeared into the void and calls remained unanswered, self-help soon turns to self-blame, as the positive paradigm turns on the unsuccessful job seeker, branding him as a "loser" in the "work-game". Rather than accepting that negativity about job searching may be a rational response to social circumstances, the message of the self-help paradigm is that your circumstances are the result of your own negativity. To challenge the ideological basis of this paradigm therefore involves a high risk of humiliation, as focusing on external obstacles leaves the individual open to accusations of being personally flawed and having a "negative attitude." Sharone describes how one Job Club attendee, after several depressing months of fruitless applications, questioned the logic of the group's upbeat discourse, which seemed to her to fly in the face of reality; in response she was asked to consider how she was "sabotaging" herself. As one expert speaker told the group, "The main barrier is yourself, not the government, not the market, it's YOU."[55]

Whether in a voluntary support group or a mandatory welfare-to-work classroom, in one form of words or another, this is the mantra which is repeatedly pushed into the head of the privatised jobseeker. The Jobcentre "customer" who is indifferent to the institutional charade of choice and positivity similarly tends to be viewed as having brought his situation upon himself. Rather than this indifference being interpreted as a justifiable response to a useless regime of compulsory advice sessions and pointless homework tasks, it is taken as a reason to intensify them: *it's no wonder you haven't got a job with that attitude.*

The end result of this prescription of self-help/self-blame and staging of jobseeking as emotional work is what Sharone calls a "depoliticization" of unemployment.[56] The shared reality is blocked in favour of an individualistic and almost evangelically positive outlook, which sees the jobseeker's destiny as being entirely in his own hands.

There is no opportunity for the emergence of supportive solidarity or of a counter-discourse that could articulate unemployment as a structural and public issue and not solely a private one, and reduce the sting of self-blame by recognising that getting a job is not entirely within the job seekers' control.[57]

Korteweg noted a similar foreclosure of collective political action in the mandatory welfare-to-work scheme for single mothers.[58] It might be argued, in fact, that such an approach produces not just depoliticized individuals but a depoliticized society, in which a narrowly individualistic and unquestioning model of self-selling is seen as the only way of formulating not only work but all social experience.

What happens, then, when the self-help/self-blame format, with its contrived positivity and subtle humiliation, comes up against a well-trodden reality, and the "work-game" is already over before it has even started? The answer is already known to those who have been through the New Deal scheme in the UK. I myself have not yet experienced one of these courses, but their reputation precedes them. The courses last thirteen weeks and are held on the private provider's own premises, where attendees are required to adhere to strict pseudo-work hours, perform supervised job searches and write set numbers of on spec letters. Unpaid work placements are also incorporated into the scheme, if these can be found. In an interview in 2009, at the time of the piloting of the latest incarnation of the scheme (the ironically named "Flexible New Deal"), Emma Harrison, boss of A4E, one of the biggest private welfare-to-work providers, said:

If you are coming on FND, it means that other interventions in the past year have not worked. You will find there will be multiple issues. That person might come with a lot of aggression, or exceptionally low self-esteem and no confidence. Unless the adviser deals with that first, then pretty much everything else we do is wasted.[59]

Here stigma is wrapped in a pseudo-therapeutic language: "low self-esteem" and "no confidence" mix with "aggression" and "multiple issues". The unemployed are pictured as both mentally weak and a physical threat, calling for a disciplinary, restraining approach, for their own sake as much as for others. A4E staff are supposedly on hand to help people deal with these "issues" (regardless of whether they are the result of a chronic lack of jobs, or being forced to attend a training course of this sort), as if they were a community mental health team offering treatment to the jobseeker, who is portrayed as a welfare addict, resistant to established "interventions".

The volatility of the capitalist economic cycle is here projected into the bodies and minds of those upon whose continued vulnerability the market depends, and which has for many years been a winning formula for Harrison's company and others in the form of government contracts and the accumulation of profit derived from public funds. A4E, in the best commercial tradition, has already been shown to run such a threadbare, target-driven New Deal "service" as to attract investigations about misleading training outcomes and reports of demoralising and under-resourced sessions.[60] One would think from such set-ups that aggression and depression were the desired outcomes of such programmes, rather than obstacles to their success.

The UK welfare system is soon due to be overhauled again by a government supposedly guided by the "new politics" of fairness and coalition. Rather than a more tolerant approach (the sort of tolerance recently accorded, for instance, to the banking sector) towards the social reality of rising unemployment, however, this is likely to result in a ratcheting up of the help-/blame-yourself rhetoric. Seemingly oblivious to the real ratio of jobs to applicants, the Conservatives plan to "Get Britain Working" through an intensified welfare-to-work schedule. The New Deal is to be re-launched as a "Work Programme" (attendance mandatory after six months on benefits) and once again will be delivered by private operators on a payment-by-results basis. Other future attractions include "Work Clubs" providing "mentoring, skills training and help to find local job opportunities", and "Service Academies" offering courses and work placements in industries such as "hospitality and leisure".[61] This last initiative might be otherwise known as "undercutting the minimum wage with a smile".

The new Work and Pensions Secretary is former Tory leader Iain Duncan Smith, whose Centre For Social Justice think tank has produced a series of reports on welfare reforms which are now being put into practice. In 2007 the second of these reports, after convening its focus groups and graciously allowing the unemployed to tell their stories, came to the conclusion that "the receipt of benefits should not be seen as an entitlement".[62] The Minister will probably be pleased to know that many of us are ahead of the game here; regardless of our circumstances we already expect nothing in the way of actual support from these new state-sponsored agencies, and have long since realised that under cover of its quasi-therapeutic consumer-friendly language the welfare system is being turned into a glorified workhouse.

Meanwhile the aspirational language of self-help continues to be pushed onto the jobseeker by the bonus-driven welfare-to-work tutor, and any objections to this self-selling orientation – either on ethical grounds, or because the individual just can't bring himself to "do it" – sound like excuses for idleness or signs of deviance. If he cannot fully embrace such a discourse and become his own salesman, then the applicant must at least simulate it in order to pass as satisfactory. The idea is presumably that by being forced to perform the role even the queerest jobseeker will eventually come to inhabit the character. Surface acting will give way to deep acting, and eventually the act itself will seem perfectly natural.

Jobseeking as Career

So the welfare state is giving way to privatised training courses and "work for the dole" schemes, while the job of jobseeking yields ever more precarious and intermittent work. From the responsibilities of the Jobcentre customer to the self-marketing duties of the unpaid intern, from the agency worker on permanent standby to the Virtual Assistant in search of virtual clients, the distinction between employment and unemployment seems increasingly arbitrary. While their formal differences are maintained by a border-patrolling bureaucracy, in terms of (lack of) content they are approaching a point of convergence. The new privatised version of unemployment has its own job description, person specification and disciplinary framework, so that if you do not perform your jobseeking duties correctly you can be fired by your line manager. Meanwhile for many employees the old-fashioned purposeful social activity of work has been replaced by a similarly privatised and professionalised form of jobseeking-on-the-job, a vocation which is attended to not only in the act of "looking busy" and selling oneself to the boss during work hours, but also by scrolling through vacancies and filling in applications during downtime and the paren- thetical hours of commuting. Jobseeking has become something abstract, an entire worldview such as used to be provided by the structure of work itself. And under the conditions of precarity and short-term insecurity, this work never ends.

The situation is illustrated by opening at random any one of the relentless torrent of CV-building self-help manuals: "The world of work is changing fast. . . . We are all applying for jobs more frequently in an increasingly competitive environment. Job-search skills that we used to need only at the start of a long period with one employer now need to be regularly sharpened and practised."[63] Jobseeking is an exercise regime which we are told we should all maintain, as we never know when we might have to run for our lives. The constant reorganisations of roles and workplaces, as described earlier, obviously contribute to this anxious treadmill of virtual mobility. But there is no discussion of exactly *why* this should be the case; the ultra-focused jobseeker has no time or energy for such airy-fairy concerns, and raising the issue in an appraisal or interview would be like questioning the existence of God during Holy Communion.

A key feature of this jobseeking-as-career orientation is the business of CV-grooming. I used to imagine CVs or résumés as being limited to professional performers and executives, but now apparently they are a matter for everyone, from factory workers and checkout assistants to students and the long-term unemployed. The CV is a particular sub-genre of post-Fordist autobiography, a copy-and-paste cosmetic narrative which accen-tuates the positives and papers over any cracks; ironically, at a time when continuity in work is at its weakest, one's life history must be made to seem as smooth and characterless as a shampoo advertisement. This again is a form of emotional labour, a micro-management of feeling. Can I force myself into a state of enthu-siasm as I string together various unwanted and unfulfilling jobs and inflate their personal significance, while reducing my identity to a series of bullet points? If I can, then once again, this is a triumph of style over substance. And the personal project of the CV is ongoing, never finished: as the Job Club members in Sharone's study are reminded, "writing résumés is . . . a continuous process of editing and revising".[64] These endlessly editable documents are virtual projections of ourselves as frictionless vehicles, constantly adapting and moving forward.

They bear no relation to the gridlocked reality which they try so desperately to repress: even if superficially tailored (or Taylorized?) to a specific vacancy, the result is bound to be both "personalised" and utterly anonymous.

Just as the CV is a sort of all-purpose packaging of the self, recruiters use the same sort of jargon to interpellate the jobseeker, either directly or remotely, in ways which are both absolutely generic and individually targeted, like a director throwing out a standard line to an out-of-work actor and saying, "OK, show me what you can do with this". For instance, the Reed job agency sends out regular mass emails which hail the recipient by name, incorporating her/him into relentlessly upbeat subject headers: "Ivor, make your first days as a temp stand out", "Ivor, add some variety to your working life", "Ivor, what's your next career move?" and my personal favourite: "Britain's got talent. What's yours, Ivor?"

Recruitment agencies are like the private welfare-to-work providers but without the social pretence; in their take-it-or-leave-it approach, the agencies have an open disregard for the reserve labourer which the welfare providers must keep hidden. The individual is compelled, by lack of other options, to offer himself for the agency's consideration, but the agency has no compulsion to reciprocate. Consequently, where the Jobcentre demands a performance of surface acting in which the unemployee is required to go through the motions, dealing with the agency is a matter of deep acting, of not merely following the script but nuancing and personalising it. As shown by their publicity materials which feature an ever-changing cast of up-for-anything guys and flexible IT girls, agencies promise utter detachment from the *content* of work, which appears to exist in a social vacuum, and at the same time demand absolute positive engagement with its *form*, its language of individual aspiration and presentation.

The jobseeker who successfully "plays" the agencies becomes, in Virno's terms, a virtuoso, selecting the most suitable elements from that generic communicative repertoire which resonates across the contemporary globalised work-space. The old skills of craftsmanship or technical proficiency are now secondary, even in manual occupations, to the new skill of linguistic and semiotic virtuosity, a kind of *stagecraft*: being able to adapt to whatever environment and identity one is thrown into and improvise a role around its unwritten rules of costume, gesture and language. A sort of verbal dexterity, the "gift of the gab", which in the Fordist era would have been associated with sales work or with working one's way deliberately up the career ladder, is now generalised and compulsory in interviews and trial periods and then in the job itself. If the old Fordist factory worker is seen as having a minor role in a long-running serial, then the post-Fordist agency actor skips from one advertisement to the next, following the circular narrative of the digital network rather than the old linearity of the production line.

The endless unpaid duties assigned to the virtuoso jobseeker cast him as the postmodernised inversion of the 1980s "gizza job" persona, which confronted the employer directly with the physical reality of the reserve labourer and his family. Now, rather than proclaiming his jobless status the career jobseeker hides it, like something obscene, behind a screen of training courses and voluntary work and expressions of rictus positivity, and he becomes ever more complicit with this concealment in proportion to his desperation. The jobseeker must have an alibi ready to explain away every gap in his employment history, while the most mundane experience becomes the occasion of a personal epiphany: "working in a busy café really taught me something about the importance of customer service." Skills are valued over knowledge. Non-vocational qualifications are almost a liability, unless they are emptied of content; a degree in literature is valued not for its evidence of critical thought but because it shows that the applicant has word processing experience.

What are we not thinking about during all those hours of jobseeking, networking and CV-building? What interests, worries and fantasies might we otherwise have? What books might we read (other than self-help manuals), what conversations might we have with colleagues and friends about topics other than work? How differently might we perceive our current jobs without this constant needling insecurity? What kind of dangerous spaces might open up, in what kind of jeopardy might we put ourselves and this dynamic system, if we resigned from our jobs as jobseekers?

Mind the Gap

I

Two months after being made redundant I got a three month temporary job, again as a warehouse assistant. The company presented itself as a small close-knit business, with directors, designers, managers, sales executives and office and warehouse staff all based in the same building. During the busy period from September to December two extra temporary warehouse workers were added. The recession apparently hadn't yet claimed this corner of the market so this year was business as usual.

In my first week as one of these temps I was invited to the annual company team-building day. After a morning picking orders and putting stickers on boxes I joined the other employees at a nearly leisure centre where a buffet was laid out and alcohol provided, and various daft games had been devised for the staff to play. From my view on the sidelines the event was reminiscent of old footage of sunny works outings, maintaining the image of the company as traditional, caring and family-friendly. It was certainly a contrast to the barely contained hostility of my previous workplace. I felt somewhat estranged from the in-jokes and social niceties, but the regular staff of all departments seemed to genuinely enjoy the occasion (all the more so as the alcohol intake increased).

But these cheerful informalities took little account of the geographic and economic realities of the business. For instance, all the actual products were manufactured in a factory in China and shipped across the world to the UK in containers before being driven here for eventual unloading and distribution. I had no idea how many people were employed in the Chinese factory, under what conditions, or what sort of hours they worked. Their wages would certainly be a tiny proportion of ours, a cold hard economic fact which formed the foundation for the entire structure of the company, as taken for granted as the warehouse floor under our feet. How did my Chinese co-workers feel about their jobs? Did they resent our apparent freedoms? Did they have their own compulsory fun days? Every day we passed the same products between us, climbed in and out of the same containers, but there was no way of communicating. This only occurred at an executive level. I once overheard the managing director talking to the warehouse supervisor about a recent trip to China. Must be an interesting place, the supervisor had said. Not where the factory is, the MD replied, just acres and acres of industrial complexes. (No, I thought, that *does* sound interesting.)

Another time I found a piece of paper lying around which appeared to be a photocopy of a close-up photograph of a product on a conveyor belt with figures partly visible behind it. The picture was meant to illustrate the right way to fix a label onto a box, I was told when I asked a colleague about it. But the photo wasn't taken here, I said, it must have been taken inside the factory in China! Look, I can see someone's elbow! He agreed, but seemed unimpressed. And that's as close as I came to getting to know my Chinese comrades.

Then there were the peripheral local workers called upon by the company as needed. On my first day I asked after the where-abouts of the other seasonal temp and was told he had found another, more permanent job. Eventually a replacement was found, but he disappeared a month later. A series of workers were then recruited via an agency for periods of between two days and three weeks. One worker told me he was telephoned by this agency at 9am and asked to start at 10am, after another worker had failed to turn up. The agency workers were paid the minimum wage (then £5.80 per hour compared to my £6.25, which was less again than the pay of the permanent staff).

The idea of covering seasonal fluctuations from within the company rather than from outside was of course unthinkable. Only when an order was incomplete and literally due to be driven away – and a potentially lucrative contract was in jeopardy – would senior staff help out, while the rest of us would be expected to work at an inhuman rate. Behind the façade of teamwork was a heap of good old fashioned profit. As we stood in a corner of the warehouse unpacking and re-packing boxes at top speed in a postmodernised pastiche of actual production, I put on a tone of mock motivational vigor and exhorted my fellow temp to "think of the managing director's Mercedes parked outside and remember the real reason why we're doing this."

At a yet further remove, when the company had a particularly labour-intensive order to fulfil they would use an outside operator, referred to only as "Steve", who would arrange for packing work to be completed off-site by his own workforce and then returned to the warehouse. While we were playing our team-building games, Steve's workers – whose conditions would probably make our own seem majestic in comparison – were presumably on an industrial estate somewhere dealing with the day's backlog from this or some other similar firm.

So beyond the friendly football banter and periodic team talks, which glued together the core workforce and helped to convey a positive brand identity along with the company's products, were various layers of satellite labour; from the factory in China, through the temporary workers like myself, to the agency recruits and the workers employed by "Steve".

In such circumstances I felt fortunate to be directly employed, and especially to have the luxury of paid days off to put aside for interviews. However, my own temporary status also had subtly demoralising and disempowering effects. For instance I was not deemed important enough to be shown how to use the warehouse database, so every time stock I was due to pick was missing I had to ask someone to look up its location for me, rather than do this myself. When I had to take something to the offices upstairs I never knew people's names or where their desks were so had to ask, as if I were a visitor. And while we cheered each other along though the unloading of another container or a session of monotonous barcode-stickering by looking forward to the Christmas shutdown and plans for last-day hilarity, such conversations were to me purely hypothetical, as I would be gone three weeks before this. These things accumulate in the mind of the temporary worker, forming a vague underlying sense of not-belonging which even the friendliest colleagues cannot shift, a weight which is carried from one workplace to the next.

Indeed, knowing that my position was temporary, I could not afford to shirk my jobseeking duties while working there, and much of my spare time was spent trying to fix up a follow-on job. Of course this was not a matter of planning my next career move, looking for inspiration, or making any sort of positive lifestyle choice. I applied for anything I thought I could get: permanent, temporary or "ongoing", industrial, retail, admin, education, care work, ranging from the substantial to the so-tenuous-as-to-barely-exist. Applying for a job at a mental health charity involved listing ten years of work history, explaining all gaps. In my case this meant twelve employers, three educational courses and seven periods of unemployment, all of which would have to be verifiable, regardless of the obligatory Criminal Records check. This is usual for jobs in the care sector, and is a daunting and depressing task for the career temp, involving hours of stitching together dates, names and addresses into a patchwork narrative guaranteed to put off even the most sympathetic potential employer. But then not to apply for such "serious" jobs is to risk typecasting oneself. In this case I reached the interview stage but was unsuccessful, possibly due to my lack of recent experience (or perhaps my trail of non-jobs). Meanwhile I also phoned up about a part-time cleaning job and was told, after giving no information beyond my phone number, that if I didn't hear back in two weeks my application had been unsuccessful; as if an analysis of these digits would constitute the entire selection process. I was interviewed for a job as a part-time shelver at a university library, but as I wasn't a student and lived several miles from the university I probably wasn't the ideal candidate. I applied for pre-Christmas work at a Tesco supermarket and upon returning their call from work on my mobile phone, was asked to attend an interview that same afternoon, which would have involved going AWOL from the warehouse. I explained that this would not be possible, but no alternative appointment was available. So this also came to nothing.

Had I been offered any of these jobs I would have had no option but to leave the warehouse before the end of my contract, and this also lent my position there a certain precariousness. Nevertheless there was a moment, after a month or so, as I sat on a wall waiting for the always-slightly-late bus home, when I realised that I had stumbled into a kind of recognisable daily rhythm. After the dread and strangeness of another new start I had begun to get to know my immediate colleagues, and felt able to exchange jokes, interests and insults with them. As crushingly dull as the actual work was, this social aspect was rewarding. I knew roughly what my job would involve from one day to the next; after the initial aches and strains my muscles had adapted themselves once again to the tasks of lifting boxes and dragging pallets, and my mind had adapted itself to the passing of time. What I had identified within myself as I waited for the bus was a certain bodily and mental imprint of regular predictable work, an emerging familiarity.

In two months, if not sooner, I would leave, and these barely formed memory impressions would be wiped in readiness for another assignment.

II

It is 6.30am and I am trying to find my way out of a multi-storey car park. I push the rubbish barrow toward the exit, past a few overnight cars. I have to report back here – to an unmarked storage cupboard on an upper floor which holds the Council's street cleaning equipment – at 1.10pm. Having arrived at the Council Depot at 6am, I was driven here and dropped off outside, and had wandered up the concrete ramp to find the shift supervisor. He spent a few minutes looking for a laminated map of my "route" – which every street cleaner should be given – but this had disappeared, so he tried to explain which streets I should clean by gesturing around the deserted car park. These instructions would of course make no sense to me once I was outside the building. I have hardly walked around this part of the city before, let alone cleared litter in it, and I have no real idea of where I'm going. I am missing a lot of the equipment I should have to do the job: as well as the map I have no litter-picking stick, as all these were taken, leaving only a broom and a shovel, and the brake on my barrow doesn't work.

Hint: just because your local "Street Cleansing Operative" happens to be wearing a Council uniform, that doesn't necessarily mean he is employed by the Council. I am hired by a private agency contracted by the Council to supply extra staff for street cleaning and bin emptying. Technically I am self-employed, meaning the agency is under no obligation to employ me from one day to the next. The self-employed agency worker[65] personifies the unfreedom of the current flexible job marketplace; as if, as I wheel this faulty barrow up and down the pavements in my fluorescent tabard, clearing up yesterday's thoughtlessly dropped rubbish under the periodic remote surveillance of a Council manager, I am somehow "being my own boss".

This is my second shift, but it might as well be my first; a different route, a different supervisor whom I have never met before and will probably never see again, the same mixture of boredom and stomach-churning anxiety. My first shift was two weeks earlier, and I was phoned by the agency again two days ago and offered another single day of work. It is in fact rare for the agency to offer work even this far in advance. Once they had called at 7.30am asking if I could work that morning, presumably because someone else had not turned up; they have also rung in the late morning to ask if I can work on the same day from 2 to 10pm. When I said this was not sufficient notice, the agent's response was that such circumstances are beyond the agency's control; they can only go on "the notice the Depot gives us". If I accept work on these terms I have conceded my absolute flexibility/desperation, but if I insist upon such unreasonable stipulations I am unlikely to get much work at all. As far as the agency and the Council are concerned, it seems that these temporary workers are not worthy of the status of human labour; like the barrows they push, they are just vehicles, kept in cupboards and wheeled out whenever needed.

Under these conditions work is closed off, parenthesised, concerned only with counting down time, like holding one's breath underwater. This bears no relation to de Botton's conception of work as a lifetime of noble struggle. Neither is this a matter of the spoilt 21st century consumer-citizen complaining about employment which is not enjoyable or fulfilling: what is missing is rather the basic human structure of work. There is an utter lack of ritual, routine, relationships. All these are emptied out, leaving behind a hollow, generic type of work, or *non-work*, without a workplace, performed by workers who are inside society but not part of it.

I push the barrow along a street of office blocks, each with its own heap of spent cigarette butts, and as I sweep them onto my shovel I imagine depositing them back into their respective foyers instead of my lidless and stinking bucket. Elsewhere the grinning window displays of shops and banks communicate a tyrannical unsleeping positivity. Against this backdrop I improvise my role with the props (or lack of them) to hand, adopting the postures of the Council street cleaner while not actually being a Council employee and not particularly feeling like a street cleaner, even as I go through the motions of sweeping up the cigarette ends. An early morning pedestrian walks towards me, perhaps thinking: there is a Council street cleaner, no doubt on his usual patch, a familiar sight, yesterday's litter being cleared away, social order still in place. But this clichéd image, in which I am as much an actor as the smiling figures in the advertisements, only disguises my deep feelings of insecurity – and possibly his too.

Where I work, doing what and for whom, for how long and how much; all these co-ordinates are arbitrary to the point of absurdity. In this non-place and this non-job, I feel detached from any meaningful social identity. The distance from my "colleagues" is as vast as is the space between myself and the members of the public who will soon be standing outside their offices, tossing their cigarettes into the gutter.

III

The just-in-time temporary worker must always keep in mind that in addition to the nominal hours for which he is paid in whatever non-job, whether for a day, a week or three months, his earnings must also cover previously accrued debts, current jobseeking duties and future gaps in employment. The UK's labyrinthine welfare system – when it does not simply refuse to help people at all – is notoriously slow to accommodate irregular work, often leaving people stranded for weeks with no income during transitions between unemployment and tenuous employment.[66] So the precarious worker is regularly thrown back on his own resources or those of his partner or family, and the waves of anxiety and helplessness ripple outwards, as those resources are likely to be at best limited, at worst non-existent.

Casual labour also undermines the National Minimum Wage,

which is implemented by many employers alongside recruitment practices which surely more than compensate for its costs. Relying on short-term and outsourced work enables employers to save money on personnel expenses, sickness and holiday pay and national insurance as well as minimising actual labour-time;[67] and in addition, the conditions of such transitory and deunionised employment are less likely to be challenged and therefore improved. The true value of a pay rate just above the minimum wage – itself not to be confused with a *living wage*[68] – is only revealed when averaged out over a period of months in and out of work, during which the worker/jobseeker must still eat, live somewhere, pay bills and debts, and be available to slot into any sort of position. This arrangement not only siphons money away from the junior worker/jobseeker and towards the manager/recruiter, it also maintains a distinct power relationship between them. The temp worker is manoeuvred into the required position of flexible conformity. The boss/agency must be satisfied, jobseeking duties kept up, all offers of overtime accepted or even two jobs "juggled" simultaneously, in a sort of inverse entrepreneurism.

Temporary work is often marketed by recruiters as a lifestyle choice, but the worker stuck in a bipolar cycle of overtime and no-time is more likely to feel manipulated by forces beyond his control, just as the corporation ventriloquizes the emotional labourer. Employers are unhappy if their worker takes unscheduled time off or vanishes suddenly, conveniently forgetting that their own demands for short-term flexibility encourage exactly this sort of pattern. The applicant must often be available to attend interviews and start work immediately, regardless of whether he happens to be working elsewhere at the time. Such instances of unauthorised absence or sudden disappearance then become part of an ongoing and convenient grumbling about temps' leisurely unreliability, as if it were they who had somehow exploited the good will of the poor capitalist.

Other than a phone message asking whether I would be available from 6am to 2pm over the Easter weekend (I was visiting my mother at the time, "unfortunately"), I heard no more from the street sweeping agency over the next fortnight, during which I continued to apply for jobs and carried on the work of writing this book. One morning at 9.30am I returned from the supermarket to find another phone message, this time from a different agency I had registered with several months earlier for assembly work which had never materialised. The message offered "a day's work", starting "immediately". The call was ten minutes ago. I phoned back to be told that the vacancy had been filled. The agent asked whether I was generally available for this kind of ad hoc work, and I told her that I was not in a position to refuse anything. This was true, as my financial situation had worsened since my diva act with the first agency and I still did not qualify for any welfare benefits; but of course, by stating my situation so matter-of-factly, without any of the performative bubble-wrap expected in such exchanges, I had almost certainly ruled myself out of any such future "opportunities".

As if in retaliation, the agent then made a point of explaining to me that people have to be very much "on the ball" about accepting this sort of work. In a glossed-over sort of way she was almost telling me off for not being there ready to answer the phone. Ten minutes is a luxury the day-labourer cannot afford: I should be waiting outside the metaphorical factory gates with my boots on, every morning. If I hadn't been playing truant in Tesco I could have been on my way to a remote industrial estate by now.

Afterwards I wondered why she hadn't rung my mobile, which was already switched on at all times in case of a call from yet another agency about possible work later in the month. But it wouldn't have made any difference, because – I am ashamed to admit – I didn't even take my mobile with me to the supermarket. I was uncontactable for half an hour. I had abandoned my post.

How could I have been so irresponsible? I am a failure as a jobseeker and a citizen.

Predictable Unpredictability

Appearing now on a screen near you: "The New Politics", a production "in the national interest", featuring a cast of white male Oxbridge millionaires. Like the weary workforce of a company undergoing a change of ownership, we all gather around our TV sets (or handheld digital devices) to hear the inaugural speech by the new Chief Executive of Team UK, who lectures us on our responsibilities and says that everyone should work together for a better, fairer society, before going off to celebrate and leaving us to wonder whether we'll still have jobs next week.

For many of us the austerity recently dusted down and worn like some vintage garment by our new governors has long been a necessity, not an ethical choice, brought on by a precariousness which does not register on the scrolling news tickers but is nevertheless felt as an internal pressure nudging at the ceiling of the skull. My partner and I exist in such a state of constant instability or predictable unpredictability, always on alert, trying to outrun our own built-in obsolescence. Uncertainty has become the usual state of things. We have adapted to this artificial climate, and we know that by continuing to tolerate and survive it we are contributing towards its perpetuation and naturalisation. Like obedient citizens, we have adjusted our expectations to accommodate this insecurity. Our immersion in a 21st century global network of technological communication exists alongside a quality of life which would have been deemed unsatisfactory thirty years ago.

My Parents moved from London to Suffolk in the 1970s when my father started work at the British Telecom Research Laboratory in Martlesham; a beautiful science-fictional space-station, once emblematic of public spirited technological progress, now a monument to a privatised future. Their generation has watched the social infrastructure they painstakingly helped to build being dismantled and sold off, while at the same time having to rescue their offspring who cannot get an economic foothold. Even in our mid to late thirties, my partner and I are chronically financially insecure, always on the verge of packing up and moving back to our parental homes.

Bringing up a family on a modest income, improvising and making do, work was then a source of pride and stability, a solid base upon which to build. Now, for us, the pressure of precarity demands a new sort of virtuosity and a different outlook. I am aware that by now I have probably already worked in more different jobs (although that word tends to glorify most of these activities) than both my parents together. Work is no longer a secure base, but rather a source of anxiety and indignity, both a matter of life and death and utterly meaningless, overwhelming and yet so insubstantial it could run through our fingers. It is normal to feel under threat and undervalued, to feel snivellingly grateful to have a job, any job. We must be sure not to take work for granted and yet be willing to be taken for granted ourselves. We endure a similar level of "making do", but without the home or kids, and without the security of regular employment. We can barely live independently now. How will we be able to bring up children, or support them in similar circumstances? The future is no longer something to look forward to, but something to dread.

Again, from my family I inherited no world-shaking political beliefs, just a desire to be part of a community, to do a useful job which was not driven by private profit and to cultivate outside interests rather than be defined by a 24/7 career. Such an attitude, far from being revolutionary, used to be the norm, even a *non-*

attitude. But now the tide has come in, and anyone with such eccentric ideas finds themselves stranded way out to sea on a sandbank with the waves lapping at their feet and the vultures circling above. By maintaining the same moderate position we have become radicals by default. Smiling swimmers beckon towards us ("Come on in, the water's lovely!"), but we know that we are in a contradictory no-win situation: our future survival depends upon immersing ourselves from head to toe in an ideology which we know is poisonous.

Nevertheless, like all would-be citizens, we have aspirations. My partner dreams of a job which is not a temporary fixed-term contract and which takes her less than two hours of commuting each way; to have transport costs which are less than a month's rent (current monthly season ticket: £383); to live near enough to work to have a social life and for her working relationships not to be undermined by inter-departmental competition. Of course I no longer aspire to a fulfilling career, but I dream of having a job – any job, regardless of interest, ability or usefulness – which lasts long enough to make inroads into my ever-expanding debt; maybe even one day to start paying off my student loan from ten years ago. In the manner of a couple imagining some gleaming Utopia, we wonder what it would be like to own our own home, to go on holiday together, to reclaim the hours filled by commuting and job applications.

But then I listen to the politicians and the lifestyle gurus and I think that perhaps my situation is self-inflicted. If only I hadn't attempted to improve myself by going back into higher education – if I had learnt some practical skill to make myself easily employable, rather than fill my head with useless knowledge, or if I had spent the time between lectures doing part-time jobs rather than studying or, even worse, writing – I wouldn't now be underemployed and trapped by debt. If I had not dared to move in with my partner I would not now have to survive without welfare benefits. If only I could embrace the prospect of a career in sales or marketing (and there are so many to choose from!), I would be free once more to enjoy life. Things would be so much easier if only I would, in the words of Team UK's new CEO, "do the right thing": give up those pointless scholarly principles and just go with the corporate flow, erasing myself in the process.

This is all my "choice", of course: the current regime does not *force* people to do anything. It manufactures consent, by any means necessary. But if humiliation or hunger do eventually make me "decide" to take that first step towards helping myself, no doubt a rehabilitative training scheme will delete all that useless education and overwrite it with unthinking positivity. A stint at a Service Academy will re-program me: I will graduate with honours and become a new sort of academic, fluent in the discourse of customer satisfaction. If I follow the script and play the role assigned to me I'll be a model citizen, with a seamless CV and immaculate presentational skills, exceeding expectations and going the extra mile. I'll show how in this society of endless mobility and boundless opportunity anyone can get to "the top" with a flexible approach, a winning smile and a ruthless eye for profit. And if I ever falter or fluff my lines my Team Leader will be there to remind me: don't worry about other people or look for any big social picture. Forget all that stuff, just look after yourself. Put those books and ideas away now, their time has gone. Just look straight ahead, keep moving, and *think positive*. Or else.

Ways Out

In Herman Melville's short story "Bartleby, The Scrivener" (1853), negation is taken to its ultimate conclusion in the employee's single, repeated phrase: "I would prefer not to."[69] The story, narrated from the point of view of a somewhat complacent employer who believes that "the easiest way of life is the best", hinges on the relation between Bartleby and his boss, and specifically the boss's growing involuntary – indeed from his own point of view absurd – sense of responsibility for this recalcitrant scribe, an attachment which is obscurely deepened not only by his non-worker's negative preferences but by his refusal to explain them. By withholding himself, as well as his labour, Bartleby gains a certain power over the boss: he takes up residence in his conscience as well as his office.

It is unsurprising, then, that Bartleby is much admired by revolutionary philosophers and resentful workers. For most present-day employees, however, such outright refusal is not possible, not just for practical reasons (which are clearly of no interest to Bartleby himself) but because of the slippery, ungraspable dimensions of the 21st century workplace. Which is to say, if Bartleby had been an agency worker the fiction would have turned out rather differently. If one fancifully imagines a temporary data enterer who preferred not to perform the tasks assigned to him, this would present today's office manager with no such terrible insight. The boss, again following the path of least resistance, would simply shrug and acknowledge this as the worker's choice, without even questioning his reasons, and order

79

a new temp from the agency to take his place. This new Bartleby could conceivably even keep returning to the non-workplace throughout various reorganisations and changes of ownership to be gently ridiculed by successive employers, like a piece of novelty furniture. He would still perish, of course, in some indeterminate non-place, but no-one would witness his final act of rebellion other than perhaps another temporary worker, say a cleaner or security guard. There would be no-one to turn away from, except himself and his own kind. The levels of mediation and the transience which are built into temp work, as well as the informality of the flexible team, mean that direct confrontation between worker and employer is bypassed. The question then is how to short-circuit this flow of indifference, how to articulate negation in a culture from which negativity itself has been banished.

In practical terms, while union support is still strong in what remains of the public sector and major privatised industries, conventional industrial action now seems to be increasingly difficult or ineffective. To address workplace fragmentation unions must try to connect with people outside their traditional spheres, in those very tenuous jobs created by outsourcing and short-term contracts which might be perceived as a threat to their members. Meanwhile, across the realm of non-unionised work, other ways must be found of expressing that critical negativity which has been suppressed by the reversible straitjacket of unfreedom. Grand self-destructive gestures would only serve to tighten the bonds of the precarious jobseeker-performer, so attention must switch to informal, tactical exercises. In contrast to the old New Times however, the ultimate aim of such tactics,[70] as modest as they are, must be to collectively pull apart this fabric of unfreedom, and not simply to allow individuals to try to wear it more comfortably.

It is well known that the just-in-time model of work contains within itself the potential for disruption, however, as this is offset by an increased capacity for self-correction, such disruption cannot be achieved by actions formally signposted in advance, but must instead be local and informal, utilising the worker's virtuosity. Managers themselves unwittingly collude in creating these sort of opportunistic openings through their motivational language of short-term targets: as we have seen, the communicative re-programming of workplaces means that staff are regularly chivvied along by daily updates, reminders of the importance of meeting this or that deadline and how it is in everyone's interests to work together to get the job done.

This situation lent itself to an interesting, if hardly revolutionary, episode at the warehouse where I was employed for three months. During the busy season it became normal for the warehouse team to work overtime for an extra hour on most days, and although technically this work was optional (and paid at "time and a half"), it was generally assumed that all staff would participate, and certainly in my case I could not afford to turn it down. This extra hour was necessary to cover peaks in the schedule, i.e. the processing of certain orders according to the requirements of retail customers. On one occasion a particularly stupid management decision meant that part of this overtime was set aside for us to perform menial tasks for the senior staff. We were indignant at this, and in response a few of us agreed to decline that hour's "optional" overtime on the day before, once this work had already been factored into the schedule.

By declining this offer at short notice we made a collective statement which we had no means of articulating in formal terms, and which we therefore had no obligation to explain (although pressure was put on some of us to do so); we just happened to each decide to take an hour off on the same day. And because the work schedule had already been set out on the assumption of this overtime, such co-ordinated action, while minuscule in terms of time and pay, had the potential to cause a ripple of concern, if nowhere near a seismic upheaval. Pre-established company loyalties – as cemented on the team-building fun day – largely averted the confrontation, but nevertheless it prompted an admission from the supervisory staff that they had taken their warehouse colleagues for granted. Of course the temp worker might not want to get involved in such a dispute for fear of jeopardising a possible permanent position, but as my job was already strictly time-limited, the circumstances were in this case favourable.

Work which involves the distribution of emotional products requires a re-claiming of mental territory. In *The Managed Heart* Hochschild suggests that in order to avoid "burnout" (over-identification with the worked-up character at the expense of the real self), the experienced emotional labourer will often estrange herself from her role, separating public image from private identity while trying to avoid guilt at feeling insincere as a result.[71] This distancing tactic is a move in the right direction for the performative worker/jobseeker, but there is a need to go further, to externalize this estrangement between self and character into a gap between worker and customer, and to push this beyond the limits of an individual coping mechanism – which could end up actually reinforcing the scripted persona – and towards a form of oppositional communication.

In the course of discussing the importance of the avant-garde arts in questioning the established social order, Marcuse invokes the Brechtian "estrangement-effect" as a way of achieving a "dissociation" with the assumptions of everyday reality. "To teach what the contemporary world really is behind the ideological and material veil, and how it can be changed, the theatre must break the spectator's identification with the events on the stage. Not empathy and feeling, but distance and reflection are required."[72] This principle might be adapted for the ideological theatre of employment in which we are now asked to take our places as actors/workers and audience/customers. In an era where all the world of work is a stage and every employee a virtuoso performer, such distance and reflection become even more critical (in both senses).[73]

This sort of estrangement-effect would aim both to unsettle the passive experience of the customer and to encourage an internal distancing process in the worker (and each, of course, depending on the context, becomes the other). A real historical example of this might be the flight attendants who, when faced with airline customer service speed-ups would, in their words, "go into robot". By withholding the worked-up warmth they had been trained to produce and interacting with passengers in a deliberately clipped, mechanical manner, they managed to say, in effect, the opposite: "I'm not a robot" – "I'll pretend, but I won't try to hide the fact that I'm pretending."[74] Under intensified working conditions this pretence was actually forced by pressure of time, accompanied by feelings of guilt at not giving customers the service they expected. The goal therefore must be to overrule this internal authority (one's own "boss") and establish this distance as a viable tactic of protest. Once again work is analogous to the performance of a play. As Hochschild notes, rather than simply refusing to act (as in a conventional strike), the workers use the words and gestures they are given to convey a message which undermines the supposed naturalness of the performance:

the play goes on, but the costumes are gradually altered, the script is shortened little by little, and the style of acting itself is changed – at the edge of the lips, in the cheek muscles, and in the mental activities that regulate what a smile means.[75]

This draws the customer's attention to the artificiality of the exchange, its economic and cultural construction. The same principle might be applied to supposedly natural (i.e. ideological) interactions between worker and supervisor. Just as the informal disciplinary strategies which shape emotional labour and precarious work evade direct industrial action, such informal tactics cannot be confronted directly by the consumer of the emotional product – customer, manager, recruiter – without also acknowledging the staged quality of the arrangement, by which, admittedly at some risk to the worker, the illusion is broken and the ideological identification is weakened.

There is a similar need for estrangement or distancing in the matter of compliance with Jobcentre bureaucracy and welfare-to-work schemes. This might come down to actions as small as putting written or verbal quotation marks around jargon headings and phrases which have to be repeated, or signing documents in a deliberately careless way so as to suggest that one's consent is worthless. To dismiss such gestures as petty would be to underestimate the restrictions under which unemployees perform their duties and the animosity which these duties generate. While again hardly the stuff of revolution, all these are in fact efforts towards finding a language of opposition which cannot be directly articulated in a one-dimensional era of compulsory participation. Again, any institutional response – even, or especially, negative – to these actions would force an acknowledgement of the real message beneath the official language of advice, choice, customer service, etc.

Beyond the gloom of the Jobcentre, in the spotlight of the competitive jobseeking talent show, the illusion of immersive identification is vital, and scepticism must be not only unspoken but heavily disguised (unless all hope is lost, of course, in which case the pompous interviewer/manager is an open target for sarcasm). This again reflects the difference between surface acting and deep acting. As noted earlier with regard to job interviews, employers have at their disposal a whole range of convenient terms – confidence, presentation, commitment, personality – upon which to hang any ideological conflict. Indeed, such judgements are often more crucial than any real ability. Having got this far, the precarious jobseeker clearly cannot afford to step outside the spirit of the discourse. It is here that the language of *camp*, as a sort of extrovert cousin of estrangement, might come into play.

Being wary of the seductions of low culture, Marcuse and his Frankfurt School allies would probably be appalled by the idea of camp as a tactic of resistance; even its early chronicler Susan Sontag deemed it "apolitical".[76] It might rather be argued that the camp sensibility cannot be *openly* political, because it is negatively defined by its proximity to social taboos and rejected values. In this context, Richard Dyer sees camp as involving "an excessive commitment to the marginal (the superficial, the trivial)", and "a characteristically gay way of handling the values, images and products of the dominant culture". By its use of "irony, exaggeration, trivialisation, theatricalisation and an ambivalent making fun of and out of the serious and respectable",[77] camp hints at the ideological construction of supposedly natural and correct behaviour. Through impersonation and masquerade, the camp performer observes the rules and performs the roles of society while at the same time "accidentally" undermining them, by holding the pose for just a moment too long or exaggerating some stylistic detail or cliché to the point of absurdity.

Here again is the potential to re-open the distance between appearance and reality, between onstage and offstage identity. Camp's strength as a clandestine language has been diluted in recent years, due thankfully to an increased (but still incomplete) acceptance of gay relationships, but also, less pleasingly, to the proliferating media industry of kitsch-for-its-own-sake and the pornification of "glamour". The result is often a bland pseudo-camp devoid of seditious queerness, like a screen with nothing behind it. There is a need to rescue camp from the respectable realm of individualized consumption and recover its collective subcultural spirit, its sense of communicating something unspeakable. Camp could then be used as an instrument to unearth those unconscious elements which would seem to today's immersive, supposedly all-inclusive society like archaeological artefacts; conflict, outsiderness, critical detachment. Such a discovery would yield a shocking insight: that even in the current postmodern era where supposedly anything goes and everyone is in on the joke, some people are still marginalized and some things are still taboo.

It is perhaps not too outlandish to suggest that those of us for whom market penetration and thrusting self-promotional contests do not "come naturally" are seen by today's cultural authorities as the new misfits, needing to be put right by a regime of remedial schemes, self-help manuals and, if necessary, medication. To avoid such treatment there is a renewed pressure to pass as a suitable candidate, to forge a convincing CV, to play it straight while communicating, within the language of the oppressor, an illicit message which cannot be expressed outright.

There is an element of camp, then, in the tragic/ridiculous situation of the job interview in which one summons a performance of over-the-top enthusiasm for a role one neither knows nor cares about; in the deliberate inverted-commas use of a preposterous business buzz-phrase in some trivial context; or in undercutting a vital meeting with a flamboyant gesture which communicates the undue importance of costume over content. Camp's use of exaggeration and stylization, and its affinity with lost causes and cultural marginalia (the "geek", whose love of knowledge for its own sake far exceeds its instrumental or vocational use, is another kindred spirit here), might therefore be directed towards revealing the stage-managed naturalness of the aspirational script, and implying an alternative imaginative space outside its rigidly defined limits.

The lack of glamour or strangeness in current popular culture is symptomatic of the need to defamiliarize the roles handed out by the state and business scriptwriters, and rekindle hostilities between the centre and the margins. Reality TV and social media eliminate offstage space, destroying mystery and celebrating banality; art slides into decorative commerce; rebellion is commodified and marketed like a fashion brand, as in supposedly alternative rock groups whose superficial revolutionary posturing is belied by a deep musical and cultural conformity and a tiresome job-interview positivity. Former punk icons are now insurance salesmen and property developers. New cultural forms based upon "distance and reflection" rather than "empathy and feeling" are called for, to break this stalemate.

What might happen if this latent negative energy was reactivated and channelled into the circuitry of immaterial labour and virtual leisure? A possible answer is provided by the female electro-pop duo Client, who first appeared in 2002. Known by the stage-names "Client A" and "Client B", in their publicity pictures – often set against industrial backgrounds – they wear matching corporate uniforms, with their faces usually cropped or turned away, as if to highlight both their objectivized status and an attitude of non-compliance. Their tracks feature lyrics about industrialised sex and sexualized industry. In their eponymous theme tune, business jargon is recited over a sleazy synth track: "Satisfaction guaranteed ... Communications expertise ... We never say no ... We aim to please ... We're the market leaders ... Available on request ... At your service." The narrator then anticipates an empty, mechanical sexual performance, her internal monologue seemingly entirely detached from her external situation, until finally she reaches an angry realisation, and a line is drawn. "Fuck off, don't touch me there". The transaction is cancelled. I am not an instrument, I am not one of your commodities. I am not what the brochure says I am.

Next the group adopted stewardess costumes and released a single called "In It For The Money": "I'm glamour glitz and tits / Shaking those hips / I'm milking the honey / I'm in it for the money / I've got a high end job / sucking corporate cock / On my hands and knees / If you please / Just give me love / Just give me sex / Just give me money".[78] The track owes something to Heaven 17's "I'm Your Money" (1981), but is more than mere pastiche. Heaven 17 critiqued Thatcherism's sharp-suited businessmen making deals between skyscrapers; Client present an updated and feminised version of this idea. The song satirises the supposedly empowered postfeminist parade of WAGs and blogging call girls, and at the same time its deadpan hookline "Work hard – why should I?" expresses the general resentment lurking behind the smile of the emotional labourer, as personified by the all-purpose hostess living in a world of mediated hospitality where everything is on display and up for sale.

The digital network might also be appropriated as an instrument with which to disable the one-dimensional program it otherwise helps to maintain. The Internet, if it can be wrested away from the powers of mobile workplace conformity and pseudo-participatory leisure, lends itself to wonderful new opportunities for communication which again can open up a critical space and make the familiar seem strange. Camp itself is arguably already a form of virtual reality: indeed, by stepping out from behind the screen of online anonymity and putting my name to this book, I feel that in the context of the temp work market I am committing an indecent act, or at least I would be, in the extremely unlikely event that any potential employer were to actually read it.

These various tactics of resistance aim towards articulating a message of critical negativity and unavailability which must be written between the lines of the script of compulsory positivity and flexibility, hinting at possible ways out of the endless, mindless loop of work/jobseeking/leisure into which so many of us have been inducted. To short-circuit this cycle of inertia and truly move forward, we have to resist the pressure to go with the flow.

Notes

1. Stuart Hall, "Brave New World", Marxism Today, October 1988, p24. Republished in revised form as "The Meaning of New Times" along with other essays in Stuart Hall and Martin Jacques ed., *New Times: The Changing Face of Politics in the 1990s* (Lawrence & Wishart, 1989).
2. Hall, p24, 28.
3. Arlie Russell Hochschild, *The Commercialization of Intimate Life: Notes from Home and Work* (University of California, 2003), p212.
4. Hall, "Brave New World", p28-29.
5. See Nina Power, *One-Dimensional Woman* (Zero, 2009), p27-43.
6. Herbert Marcuse, *One-Dimensional Man* (Routledge, 1991 [1964]), p3-21.
7. Marcuse, p14.
8. Marcuse, p20.
9. "Creating a new public sphere, without the state", interview with Paolo Virno by Héctor Pavón, 24 December 2004. http://libcom.org/library/creating-a-new-public-sphere-without-the-state-paolo-virno
10. These include the EuroMayDay network, dedicated to organising annual protests against precarious work in European cities (http://www.euromayday.org/), and the Italy-based Chainworkers website (http://www.chain-workers.org/). The anti-precarity movement also has its own "patron saint", San Precario. See Marcello Tarì and Ilaria

Vanni, "On The Life and Deeds of San Precario, Patron Saint of Precarious Workers and Lives", in Fibreculture, Issue 5, September 2005. http://journal.fibreculture.org/issue5/vanni_tari.html

11. Angela Mitropoulos, "Precari-us?" in Mute Vol. 2 No.0: Precarious Reader (2005), p16.

12. Karl Marx, *Capital Volume 1* (Penguin, 1976), p562, 580-82, 793.

13. Although recent strikes in public sector and privatised companies in the UK have raised the profiles of some unions, this does not translate into the experience of much of the low-paid working population. Traditional union membership, for instance, does not lend itself to unstable work patterns with frequent moves, irregular income and no attachment to any particular "trade". The argument for making the kind of support historically provided by unions more accessible to precarious workers is made by Anna Pollert in *The Unorganised Vulnerable Worker: The Case For Union Organising* (Institute of Employment Rights, 2007).

14. Mitropoulos, "Precari-us?", p16.

15. Sonia McKay's *Agency and Migrant Workers* (Institute of Employment Rights, 2009) presents an excellent summary of the precarious legal situation of migrant agency workers in the UK, including those employed by gangmasters.

16. See for example McKay, p42-45, 51-52.

17. Alain de Botton, *The Pleasures and Sorrows of Work* (Hamish Hamilton, 2009), p105-129.

18. de Botton, p87-88, 256-257.

19. Arlie Russell Hochschild, *The Managed Heart: Commercialization of Human Feeling* (2nd Edition) (University of California, 2003 [1983]), p7.

20. Hochschild, p35-55.

21. Michael Hardt and Antonio Negri, *Empire* (Harvard University, 2000), p293.

22. Paolo Virno, *A Grammar of the Multitude* (Semiotext(e), 2004), p52-56.

23. Hochschild, *The Managed Heart,* p203.

24. Hochschild, p102-3.

25. See Hochschild, p153-156 for the formulation of class and emotional labour; on gender and emotional labour, see p162-184; for discussion of supermarket cashiers, see p149-150.

26. Virno, *A Grammar of the Multitude,* p91.

27. Virno, p62.

28. Marc Augé, *Non-Places: Introduction to an Anthropology of Supermodernity* (Verso, 1995), p111. Augé takes the term "non-place" from Michel de Certeau.

29. The connection between Augé's non-places and so-called "non-people" and "non-services" is made, perhaps somewhat over-simplistically, by George Ritzer in *The Globalization of Nothing* (Sage, 2004), p39-71.

30. Manuel Castells, *The Rise of the Network Society* (2nd edition) (Blackwell, 2000), p406, 407-459.

31. Augé, *Non-Places,* p103.

32. For an excellent thematic overview of this film see Kim Nicolini, "A Landscape of Impossible Options", Counterpunch, 5 February 2010. http://www.counterpunch.org/nicolini02052010.html

33. On the organisational effects of outsourcing NHS support staff to private agencies, Polly Toynbee's account of working as a porter in a London hospital is especially illuminating. See Toynbee, *Hard Work* (Bloomsbury, 2003), p55-84.

34. Castells, *The Rise of the Network Society,* p296.

35. For an analysis of this closed circuit of cyber-bureaucracy, see Mark Fisher, *Capitalist Realism* (Zero, 2009), p62-70.

36. This phrase was used by television manufacturer LG in a recent TV advertisement to convey a message of commodified freedom.

37. Raymond Williams, *Television: Technology and Cultural Form*

(Routledge, 2003 [1974]), p95. Williams' prescient study analysed the intertexual "flow" of TV, showing how it blended various and sometimes conflicting discourses into a single seductive rhythm.

38. This phrase is lifted from Anne Friedberg's *Window Shopping: Cinema and the Postmodern* (University of California, 1994), p28. In Friedberg's text it refers to the sensation of movement produced in a static viewer by the panoramas and dioramas of the 18th and 19th centuries.

39. Ian Sanders, *Juggle! Rethink Work, Reclaim Your Life* (Capstone, 2009), p5, 19, 121.

40. Woman's Hour, BBC Radio 4, 12 January 2010. http://www.bbc.co.uk/radio4/womanshour/03/2010_02_tue.s html

41. Mira Katbamna, "Homing in on the Future", Guardian, 4 July 2005. http://www.guardian.co.uk/money/2005/jul/04/careers.thegu ardian

42. "What is a Virtual Assistant?" http://www.ukava.co.uk/ Accessed 15 May 2010.

43. In a discussion of insurance industry occupations in *The Rise of the Network Society* (p266), Castells mentions the informational workplace's propensity for "ideologically tailored new [job] titles (for example 'assistant manager' instead of 'secretary')" which aim to increase the "commitment of clerical workers without correspondingly increasing their professional rewards". Of course VAs might argue that despite the insecurity, extra hours and lack of workplace support, their own professional rewards, in terms of money or status, *have* increased.

44. Jack Lanigan, *The Kingdom Did Come* (undated autobiography), cited in John Burnett, *Idle Hands: The Experience of Unemployment, 1790-1990* (Routledge, 1994), p170.

45. See Marx, *Capital Volume 1*, p781-794.

46. Wilde's essay "The Soul of Man under Socialism" (1891) remains influential in questioning the automatic usefulness of work. On this and other historical examples of resistance to the ideology of work, see Owen Hatherley, "Work and Non-Work: A Short History of the Refusal to Work as a Revolutionary Strategy", http://themeasurestaken.blogspot.com/2008/06/work-and-non-work.html 6 June 2008.

47. The above quotes are from a talk given by Jobcentre advisors at a compulsory "back-to-work" session, 9 February 2010.

48. Interpellation refers to the hailing of the individual in a particular way by an ideological authority, prompting a recognition of oneself as an ideological subject in those terms (for instance as the police officer hails a suspect). The term derives from Louis Althusser, in *Lenin and Philosophy and other essays* (Monthly Review Press, 2001 [1971]), p115-120.

49. Literally, in my case; claiming Jobseeker's Allowance in July 2009 after eleven months of continuous employment, I discovered that because my partner was working full-time and I had been a postgraduate student from September 2006-7, I was not entitled to either income- or contribution-based JSA. To become eligible for benefit would have required moving out of the flat I shared with my partner and moving into a separate bedsit, or going back to my parental home 120 miles away (breaking up cohabiting couples is a DWP speciality). For various bureaucratic reasons, however, I was advised that it was still in my interests to continue signing on and presenting my "Jobsearch Diary" for inspection, even though I was receiving no benefit.

50. Anna C. Korteweg, "Welfare Reform and the Subject of the Working Mother: 'Get a Job, a Better Job, Then a Career'", Theory and Society Vol.32 No.4 (August 2003), p445-480.

51. Korteweg, p462-466.

52. Korteweg, p468-469.

53. Ofer Sharone, "Constructing Unemployed Job Seekers as Professional Workers: The Depoliticizing Work-Game of Job Searching", Qualitative Sociology (2007), p406.

54. Sharone, p405, 407.

55. Sharone, p411-414.

56. Sharone, p404.

57. Sharone, p415.

58. Korteweg, "Welfare Reform and the Subject of the Working Mother", p472.

59. "Work in Progress", Emma Harrison interview by Amelia Gentleman, Guardian, 30 September 2009. http://www.guardian.co.uk/society/2009/sep/30/emma-hamilton-unemployment-tougher-benefits

60. See Rajeev Syal and Toby Helm, "Fraud Inquiry into Government Jobs Scheme", Observer, 28 June 2009. http://www.guardian.co.uk/politics/2009/jun/28/fraud-inquiry-government-jobs-scheme ; and Wesley Stephenson, "Jobless Training Courses 'Demoralising'", BBC News, 4 April 2009. http://news.bbc.co.uk/1/hi/uk/7982550.stm

61. "Where We Stand: Jobs and Welfare", Conservative Party, http://www.conservatives.com/policy/where_we_stand/jobs _and_welfare.aspx Accessed 16 May 2010.

62. Social Justice Policy Group, *Breakthrough Britain: Ending the Costs of Social Breakdown (Volume 2: Economic Dependency and Worklessness)*, July 2007, p90. http://www.centreforso-cialjustice.org.uk/client/downloads/economic.pdf

63. Rebecca Corfield, *Preparing the Perfect CV* (5th edition) (Kogan Page, 2010), p1.

64. Sharone, "Constructing Unemployed Job Seekers as Professional Workers", p407.

65. Agency workers are often designated as self-employed, meaning that in disputes over pay or dismissal neither agency nor client can be held legally responsible. See McKay,

Agency and Migrant Workers, p25.

66. See for instance McKay, p31-32, and Toynbee, *Hard Work*, p84.

67. See McKay, p32.

68. Church Action On Poverty, a leading campaigning organisation on the issue of low pay, calculates the UK Living Wage in 2010 at £7.14, compared to a National Minimum Wage of £5.93 (from October 2010 onwards). http://www.church-poverty.org.uk/campaigns/livingwage /livingwagebriefing2010

69. Herman Melville, *Bartleby, The Scrivener* (Hesperus, 2007 [1853]).

70. The term "tactics" here is indebted to Michel de Certeau's essay "'Making Do': Uses and Tactics", in which it is opposed to the "strategies" of powerful institutions. "The space of a tactic is the space of the other. Thus it must play on and with a terrain imposed on it and organised by the law of a foreign power." In *The Practice of Everyday Life* (University of California, 1984), p37.

71. Hochschild, *The Managed Heart*, p188.

72. Marcuse, *One-Dimensional Man*, p70.

73. Bertolt Brecht actually mentions that his "A-effect" might be witnessed in various ways "as a procedure in everyday life", as a way of defamiliarizing those exchanges which are seemingly ordinary. See the essay "Short Description of a New Technique of Acting which Produces an Alienation Effect", in John Willett ed., *Brecht On Theatre* (Methuen, 1964), p136-147.

74. Hochschild, *The Managed Heart*, p129. The image of the robotic customer service assistant might be a post-Fordist sequel to Charlie Chaplin's factory worker who becomes an unwilling physical component in the speeded-up assembly line in his 1936 film *Modern Times*.

75. Hochschild, p131.

76. Susan Sontag, "Notes On 'Camp'", in *Against Interpretation* (Vintage, 1994), p277.

77. Richard Dyer, *Heavenly Bodies: Film Stars and Society* (St.Martin's, 1986), p178.

78. In the radio-friendly album version of the track these lyrics are slightly "modified".